AN ANGEL'S GUIDE TO HEAVEN ON EARTH

Susan Ann Gossett

Angelic Mission Publishing
P. O. Box 16781
Portland, OR 97216

AN ANGEL'S GUIDE TO HEAVEN ON EARTH

ISBN 0-9632029-0-1

Library of Congress Catalog Card Number: 91-78319

First Printing, Spring 1992

Angelic Mission Publishing
P. O. Box 16781
Portland, OR 97216

Printed in the United States of America

10 9 8 7 6 5 4 3 2 1

Dedication

To my sons, Robert and Brian Caster

Believe always in yourselves and in your dreams, for you have the power to make each one happen. Never let fears or doubts, your own or anyone else's, stop you from creating your own Heaven on Earth.

Acknowledgments

I would like to thank the following people for their outstanding contribution in completing this project.

To my husband/growth partner, Chris, for being on the other side of the 'spelling wheel' so that we could communicate with Sonny and receive his messages. I also want to thank you for all of the time and energy you put into the wonderful illustrations, the beautiful book cover, and for your brilliant idea to create *Angel Talk*, the tool which enabled us to communicate with Sonny in the first place.

To Bess Anderson and Pat Jeter for choosing 'a long time ago' to be involved in this project. The growth and the experiences we have shared are too many to mention here, but thank you both so much for all of the countless hours you have put in to ensure the physical manifestation of Sonny's book.

To Berdell Moffet for sharing your professional knowledge of self-publishing with me and for suggesting such wonderful people with whom to do business.

To Toby Condon for your contribution of putting all of this on computer for me. I am sure, Toby, that you will never forget the experience!

To Aaron Friend for doing all of the corrections and for getting this book all ready for the printers.

To Barbara Wurst for doing the tedious job of editing and for all your honest feedback.

To Casey Chaney for showing me the value in taking risks.

And to my parents, Chuck and Edythe Rogers, for encouraging me to follow my own path, even at times when you didn't understand.

Thank you all for the parts you played in completing this mission. Without each of you, it would not have happened.

Table of Contents

INTRODUCTION
BY
SUSAN GOSSETT

This book was written by an Angel, named Sonny, whose mission is to deliver God's messages to the world. He delivered these messages in the form of lessons, in order for us to understand them on a more personal level. He decided to dictate these lessons through a new spiritual tool called 'Angel Talk', which is explained later in the introduction. The lessons that Angel Sonny has given us are all ongoing lessons. They are actually techniques that you can use all of your life. The lessons are very workable and really fun to do. They can be done individually or in a group. All of the lessons are given to you in Angel Sonny's exact words just as he dictated them.

It was in 1987 that Angels became really important in my life. My husband, Chris, and I had purchased a book which explained how to contact the angelic realm. We practiced the techniques described in the book and made our connections. It was only a few weeks later that Chris and I made our first trip to Peru. We took our Angels with us and due to many unforeseen circumstances there, we had to call upon them numerous times to help us. Our connection with them grew very strong.

After returning from that trip, Chris and I wanted so much to talk directly to the Angels who had become so important to our lives. We tried the Ouija board first, but our experiences with it did not bring the results we had hoped. We were communicating mostly with what Sonny refers to as 'The Playful Bunch'. The playful bunch are those spirits on the astral plane. We had some fun with them, but what we really wanted to do was talk to our Angels. The idea came to Chris to make his own version of a talking board. We wanted to make the energies of the board more conducive to the higher vibrations. So, thus 'Angel Talk' was born. We later learned that Chris' idea to make his own board was given to him by Sonny so that we would have a tool through which to communicate.

It was April of 1990 that Sonny first came to us. There were three of us that evening. Chris and I worked the board while our friend, Pat Jeter, wrote down all the information we were receiving. Sonny came to us that evening to give us insights and information about some of the situations we were dealing with in our lives.

After a few more sessions with Sonny, we decided to invite another friend, Bess Anderson, to join us. We did not know at the time Sonny was behind our invitation. As the session began that evening, Sonny came through with the following: "*WELL, I SUPPOSE THAT YOU ARE WONDERING WHERE THIS IS ALL HEADING. WELL, I ASSURE YOU THAT I WILL NOT LEAD YOU ASTRAY. WOULD YOU ALL LIKE TO BE IN ON A LITTLE SECRET? I HAVE BEEN PREPARING YOU ALL TO RECEIVE MY MESSAGES AND TO GIVE MY MESSAGES TO OTHERS. THE PROJECT YOU HAVE CHOSEN TO COMPLETE INVOLVES MY DICTATION, YOUR EXPERIENCES WITH THE LESSONS THAT I WILL BE GIVING TO YOU, AND THE CHANGES YOU WILL MAKE IN YOUR REALITIES AFTER COMPLETING THE LESSONS. WHAT YOU DO WITH THE MATERIAL IS TOTALLY UP TO YOU, BUT A BOOK FORM WOULD BE MOST PLEASING TO ME. YOU COULD CALL IT WHATEVER YOU COLLECTIVELY DECIDE.*" Well needless to say, we were truly shocked and amazed at the project we were about to undertake. For several minutes, we just sat there in silence. What had started out as a fun evening was the beginning of something we were yet to comprehend.

We all wanted to know how we had been chosen for such a project. Sonny explained it to us in this way: "*YOU EACH WERE CHOSEN LONG AGO, BEFORE THIS LIFETIME. IT HAS TAKEN THIS LONG TO GET BACK TOGETHER AGAIN. FOR MOST OF YOUR LIVES, YOU HAVE BEEN GENTLY GUIDED TO PEOPLE AND CIRCUMSTANCES WHICH WOULD PREPARE YOU TO BE OPEN ENOUGH TO APPRECIATE MY MESSAGES, METHODS, AND HUMOR. GUIDANCE YOU HAVE RECEIVED THROUGH THE YEARS IS TOO MUCH TO MENTION, BUT LOOK BACK OVER YOUR PAST AND YOU MAY FIND SOME OF YOUR BEST DECISIONS MAY HAVE BEEN PROMPTED BY 'YOURS TRULY'. THE NUMEROUS PAST LIVES YOU HAVE SHARED IS RELEVANT, YET INSIGNIFICANT. I WILL SAY, THOUGH, THAT YOU FOUR HAVE CERTAINLY TRIED*

GOD'S PATIENCE, BUT YOU HAVE ALSO PLEASED HIM GREATLY." We began meeting for sessions with Sonny twice weekly and sometimes even more frequently. We were so excited about this project and we just couldn't stay away from it for too long. Sonny was so much fun and we always felt so good whenever we talked to him. Time just flew by! Knowing that we were actually talking with an Angel was just so exciting! Our sessions were always full of laughter and our energies were high. Sonny has a way of making you feel as if you are on top of the world. Sonny's energy is always loving even when he is telling you something that you would rather not hear. We always felt wonderful after the sessions were over.

Each of us had a role to play during our sessions. Chris and I would sit at our 'Angel Talk' board and put our hands on the wheel which would point to the letters on the board. Bess would sit next to us and read the letters as they were spelled out. Pat's job was to write down all the information as it came through. Doing it this way made our sessions flow easily and quickly. (Too quickly!) Sometimes Sonny would have to remind us to stop for the evening and rest.

'The Fabulous Four' with portrait of Sonny. Standing left to right, Pat Jeter and Bess Anderson. Seated holding Angel Talk Board, Chris and Susan Gossett

You may be wondering how Sonny was able to transmit to us through our 'Angel Talk' board. We were curious about that too, and asked him that question. This is how he explained it: "*I SEND THOUGHTS TO YOU AND YOUR MIND RECEIVES THE THOUGHTS LIKE AN ANTENNA RECEIVES RADIO SIGNALS. YOU MAY SOMETIMES HEAR THE WORDS FIRST IN YOUR HEAD AND THAT IS ALRIGHT. THEN THE SIGNALS ARE TRANSLATED INTO NERVE IMPULSES WHICH TRIGGER YOUR HANDS TO MOVE.*

THUS IS A MESSAGE SENT AND RECEIVED. SOME PEOPLE OF FINELY TUNED RECEPTABILITY CAN PICK UP HIGH VIBRATIONS WITH GREAT CLARITY, SUCH AS THE TWO IN GREAT HARMONY AT THE WHEEL HERE". It made sense and explained why our hands and fingers would sometimes tingle.

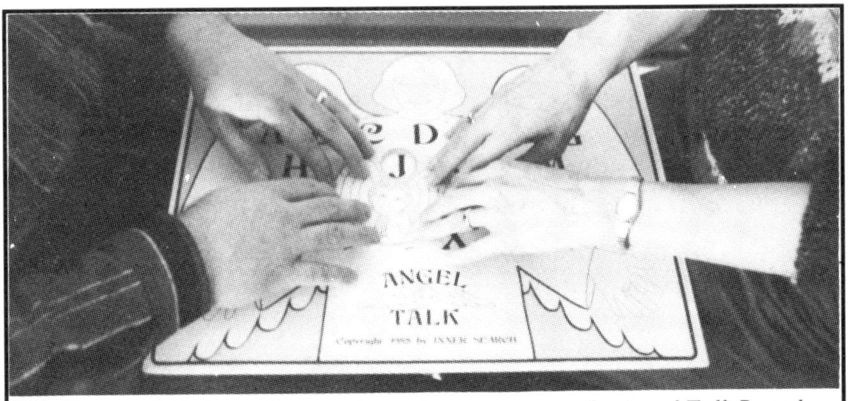

Susan and Chris spelling out Sonny's messages on the Angel Talk Board

We were also very curious how he got his name. Here is his answer: "*SONNY WAS THE NAME GIVEN ME BY THE ELDER ANGELS, AS AN ENDEARING TERM, TO SIGNIFY THAT I CAME INTO BEING AS AN ANGEL MUCH LATER THAN THEY. BEFORE THAT I WAS MERELY A PART OF THE 'ALL THAT IS', WITHOUT INDIVIDUALITY. I STUDIED PEOPLE FOR CENTURIES AND THEN WAS FINALLY GIVEN A MISSION, AND YOU ARE IT, AND NOW I HAVE A PURPOSE. MY PURPOSE IS TO INTERACT WITH YOU DIRECTLY TO COMPLETE THIS PROJECT AND GIVE IT TO THE WORLD. AND IF I HAVE DONE WELL, I AM ASSURED THE OPPORTUNITY TO WORK FURTHER WITH PEOPLE TO HELP THEM GROW SPIRITUALLY*".

Something very exciting happened one evening during one of our sessions and I would like to share it with you. It happened right after we had received our third lesson. Out of the blue, Sonny asked us if there was something he could do to prove his authenticity. We did not know what to ask of him so he asked if we would like to see him. Well, that shocked us because it was the last thing we expected. We immediately asked him if he could really do that. He said, "*SORT OF, I HAVE*

NO PHYSICAL BODY, BUT PERHAPS I COULD PRODUCE A SMALL LIGHT SHOW FOR YOU." We turned off all of the lights and to our amazement the show began. A beautiful light started to come out of a bowl that contained a picture of Sonny. It went from there to the counter in the kitchen where it danced all around and then jumped into a roll of paper towels where it illuminated out in all directions. From there it danced into the hall where it grew to the size of a small person. The lights coming from it looked like the Aurora Borealis. When it was over, we were speechless. These are Sonny's comments afterwards: "*DID YOU ENJOY MY LIGHT SHOW? I NEED TO EXPLAIN THAT SINCE MY LIGHT IS NOT VISIBLE TO PHYSICAL EYES, I BORROWED SOME BEAUTIFUL SUNLIGHT AND CAUSED IT TO DANCE AROUND-THUS A LIGHT SHOW WAS PRODUCED.*"

You will find throughout this book Chris' drawings of Sonny to further explain each lesson. We have enjoyed working with Sonny and helping him get his book together. It truly has been a learning experience.

Sonny has asked me to tell you that he and others will be there to help you through each of your lessons. His mission with us is completed and his next mission is to help all of you. He said not to hesitate to ask for help whenever you need his assistance. We hope that you all will enjoy reading and working the lessons and getting to know Sonny as we have. We would love to hear about your experiences and the changes you make in your life. Be prepared for lots of laughter and for the unexpected!

For Sonny

There is an Angel,
whose name is Sonny.
He became our friend,
and is really quite funny.

He gives us love
and laughter galore,
and helps us see
what we are here for.

The message he brings,
is really quite clear.
Lighten your life with God
and His Angels
and be of good cheer!

Lovingly,
Bess

HI, I AM SONNY

INTRODUCTION
BY
ANGEL SONNY

IT IS NO MERE COINCIDENCE THAT THIS BOOK IS IN YOUR HANDS; YOU WERE GUIDED TO IT. YOU ARE READY TO EMBARK UPON A MOST SPLENDID JOURNEY OF PERSONAL AND SPIRITUAL UNFOLDMENT.

EVERY SO OFTEN GOD SENDS ANGELS, HIS MOST IMMEDIATE CONTACTS TO PEOPLE, TO DELIVER MESSAGES. THE CONTENT IS HIS, HOWEVER, HE LET ME DELIVER IT IN WHATEVER WAY I CHOSE AND TO WHOMEVER I CHOSE. I CHOSE TO DELIVER GOD'S TIMELY MESSAGES IN THE FORM OF LESSONS. I CHOSE FOUR WONDERFUL PEOPLE TO RECEIVE THE LESSONS THROUGH MY DICTATION AND TO EXPERIENCE THEM WORKING IN THEIR LIVES. THESE FOUR, WHOM I CALL 'THE FABULOUS FOUR', DECIDED TO CALL THIS COLLECTED BODY OF MATERIAL 'AN ANGEL'S GUIDE TO HEAVEN ON EARTH'. SO THIS BOOK CONTAINS MY DICTATION OF GOD'S MESSAGES AND THE 'FABULOUS FOUR|S' EXPERIENCES WITH THE LESSONS, ALONG WITH A

LOT OF ANGEL HUMOR AND OTHER INTERESTING AND USEFUL INFORMATION.

THE MESSAGES GOD GAVE ME TO DELIVER ARE SIMPLE AND BASIC. THEY ARE GOD'S 'TEN REMINDERS'. THEY GO AS FOLLOWS:

REMEMBER:

1. THAT I ALWAYS LOVE YOU JUST AS YOU ARE, NO MATTER WHAT.

2. TO LOVE AND APPRECIATE YOURSELF AND ALL OTHERS.

3. THAT LIFE IS A GIFT AND IT IS YOUR CHOICE HOW YOU LIVE IT.

4. THAT YOU HAVE THE POWER TO CHANGE YOUR LIFE.

5. THAT YOU DESERVE EVERY GOOD THING THAT LIFE HAS TO OFFER.

6. THAT THE PURPOSE OF LIFE IS TO CREATE, EXPERIENCE, LEARN, GROW, AND TO HAVE FUN WITH IT ALL.

7. THAT THE UNIVERSE NEEDS YOU AND SUPPORTS YOU IN FULFILLING YOUR PURPOSE.

8. THAT SPIRITUAL GUIDANCE IS ALWAYS AVAILABLE AND ALL ANSWERS ARE WITHIN YOU.

9. THAT EVERYTHING YOU WANT OR NEED IS YOURS IN ABUNDANCE.

10. TO LAUGH OFTEN.

I DO BELIEVE THAT I DID QUITE WELL IN CAPTURING THE ESSENCE OF GOD'S MESSAGES IN FORTY MARVELLOUS LESSONS. THEREFORE IT IS WITH GREAT JOY AND LOVE THAT I PRESENT TO YOU 'AN ANGEL'S GUIDE TO HEAVEN ON EARTH'.

ARE YOU NOT TERRIBLY EXCITED? CAN YOU HARDLY WAIT? THEN LET US PREPARE FOR LOTS OF CHUCKLES AS YOU FIND IT IS FUN TO GROW.

LESSON 1

REAL AND UNREAL - REAL IS JUST A THOUGHT AWAY

TO BEGIN WITH, I WOULD LIKE TO CAUTION YOU THAT SOME OF THE CONCEPTS THAT WE WILL BE WORKING WITH MAY SEEM STRANGE TO YOU. THIS IS BECAUSE YOU HAVE BEEN TRAINED TO BELIEVE IN ILLUSIONS AND NOW YOU ARE IN THE PROCESS OF SEEING THROUGH THOSE ILLUSIONS TO THE TRUTH BEHIND THEM. FIRST OF ALL, THE THINGS THAT YOU SEEM TO THINK ARE REAL AND THE THINGS YOU THINK ARE UNREAL ARE THE SAME THINGS. THE QUITE SIMPLE PROCESS THEN, OF LEARNING THE DIFFERENCE, IS ELIMINATED. BY THAT, THERE IS NOTHING TO LEARN EXCEPT THIS FIRST RULE: REAL AND UNREAL ARE THE SAME THING.

EACH TIME THAT YOU DISPEL A MYTH ABOUT REALITY, AS YOU WERE TRAINED TO PERCEIVE IT, YOU COME CLOSER TO MORE FULLY UNDERSTANDING THE SECRET BEHIND REALITY CREATION. I WANT TO EMPHASIZE THAT REAL AND UNREAL ARE MADE UP LITERALLY IN YOUR

HEAD. YOU GET TO CHOOSE WHAT YOU WANT TO BE REAL. IT IS THAT SIMPLE. FOR INSTANCE, YOUR THOUGHTS HAVE TOTALLY CONVINCED YOU THAT YOU ARE WHAT YOU ARE AND THAT YOU HAVE WHAT YOU HAVE. YOU EITHER HAVE THIS, OR YOU DO NOT. YOU DO THIS FOR A LIVING, OR YOU DO NOT. YOU CAN DO THIS, OR YOU CAN NOT. CHANGING YOUR THOUGHTS WILL CHANGE WHAT YOU HOLD AS REAL.

GO OUT INTO THE WORLD, THE STREETS, A STORE, YOUR WORK PLACE, AND PLAY MAKE-BELIEVE. MAKE-BELIEVE YOU HAVE A LOT OF MONEY IN THAT BANK OVER THERE, OR YOU WORK THERE, OR BETTER YET YOU OWN IT! YOU ALSO OWN THAT CAR AND THAT STEREO AND THAT HOME AND WHY NOT, YOU JUST WON THE LOTTERY! IT IS ALL JUST A THOUGHT AWAY.

IT IS YOUR THOUGHTS ABOUT THINGS THAT BRING THEM INTO YOUR REALITY. THIS IS ALSO TRUE WITH YOUR THOUGHTS ABOUT PEOPLE. YOU CAN SAY, THAT IS MY FRIEND OVER THERE, OR THOSE PEOPLE IN THE BUILDING ALL LOVE ME DEARLY. SO PLAY MAKE-BELIEVE FOR A WHOLE WEEK AND HAVE FUN. NOTICE HOW YOUR FEELINGS OF LACK AND SCARCITY DISAPPEAR. NOTICE ALSO, YOUR INCREASED SENSE OF WELL-BEING AND PROSPERITY.

IF YOU HAD ONE THOUSAND DOLLARS, AN AMAZON RIVER NATIVE WOULD SAY THAT YOU ARE RICH, WHILE A MILLIONAIRE WOULD NOT. IT IS ALL IN HOW YOU LOOK AT IT. IF YOU OWN A BANK, WHO IS TO SAY THAT YOU DO NOT, EXCEPT FOR SOMEONE WHO DOES NOT SHARE YOUR THOUGHTS.

REMEMBER BELIEVING IS SEEING AND YOU ARE ONLY AS ABUNDANT OR DESTITUTE AS YOU WANT TO BELIEVE, REGARDLESS OF WHAT YOUR ILLUSION OF REALITY WANTS TO SHOW YOU. CHOOSE TO BELIEVE YOU HAVE ALL YOU WANT, IT IS ONLY THE FLIPSIDE OF THE ILLUSION AND IT IS MORE FUN!

IF YOU NO LONGER WANT TO LIVE UNDER THE BELIEF THAT YOU ARE POOR, UNEMPLOYED, AND UNLOVED - REMEMBER THAT A NEW REALITY IS JUST A NEW THOUGHT AWAY.

SUMMARY

LESSON 1

This first lesson was, and still is, a very difficult one for us to understand. To understand it in our heads was easy enough, but to really understand the concept as it applied to our own physical lives was another thing entirely. We had always believed that there was a difference between what was real and what was unreal. In our studies of metaphysics, we have always heard that belief precedes reality, but now it was time to test that concept.

I had an interesting experience after this lesson. I woke up the next morning feeling strange in my surroundings. Everything seemed unfamiliar to me. It was as if I was in a strange apartment in a foreign country and I was experiencing culture shock. This is the best way that I know to describe it. I have lived here for the past seven years, yet nothing about it was familiar to me. I am sure that it was to show me what Sonny was trying to tell us.

Playing make believe was really fun. It helped us to look at our belief systems. It really helped us to be aware of the thoughts we entertain. We were starting to understand how our thoughts relate to the physical reality that we create. We all seemed to have better luck playing make-believe with people than we did with anything else. We saw positive results with how people responded to us when we played make-believe with them. As an example, one evening Bess and Pat went out to dinner. Bess had been to a photographer and was wearing an elegant and expensive dress with pearls. The waiter automatically assumed that she was a celebrity. Bess seized the opportunity to play make-believe. During the course of dinner, the manager came by several times to make sure that everything was satisfactory. Upon leaving, she commented she was waiting for her limo, even turning to look for it. The manager believed her. As they were leaving, the manager asked Pat to bring her friend back again. Later in the car Bess and Pat roared with laughter.

Working on changing our thoughts is a continual effort. It takes time for physical reality to show us our new thoughts and sometimes getting impatient, our old thoughts creep back in. But we are aware now how it works and we are working hard to dispel our old way of thinking. We help each other with this by listening to each other's conversation and making each other aware when we hear an old belief spoken. Everyday we are getting better at recognizing when old beliefs are creeping back and we remember what it is we really want to create with our thoughts.

When we go out and play the make-belive game, we notice a big change in the way we feel. We feel happy and powerful. We are able to let go of all of our worries and replace them with hope.

LESSON 2

LOVE IS THE ESCALATOR TO ENLIGHTENMENT

EVERY TIME YOU FEEL LOVING, YOU RAISE YOUR VIBRATION. AS YOU RAISE YOUR VIBRATION, YOU GET CLOSER TO ENLIGHTENMENT. LOVING FEELINGS COME FROM AN OPEN HEART. YOU CAN OPEN YOUR HEART BY LOVING YOURSELF. LOVING YOURSELF MEANS ACCEPTING AND HONORING THE FACT THAT YOU ARE OKAY.

THIS LESSON CALLS FOR YOU TO LOVE EVERYTHING ABOUT YOURSELF, ESPECIALLY THOSE THINGS YOU HAVE JUDGED AS WRONG, NEGATIVE, OR BAD. IT IS EASY TO LOVE YOURSELF WHEN YOU FEEL YOU ARE DOING SOME-THING GOOD, HAVING POSITIVE EMOTIONS, AND MAKING GOOD DECISIONS THAT WORK OUT WELL. BUT WHAT ABOUT WHEN EVERYTHING YOU TOUCH FALLS APART, WHEN EVERY CHOICE YOU MAKE SEEMS WRONG, AND ALL YOU FEEL IS FEAR, DOUBT, AND ANGER? LOVE YOURSELF

AND THOSE FEELINGS. THE WORST THING YOU CAN DO IS JUMP ALL OVER YOURSELF WITH JUDGEMENTS LIKE; "I AM AWFUL. I AM A FAILURE, I AM NO GOOD, I CAN NOT," ETC. TRY FOR A CHANGE TO MENTALLY SAY "STOP", AND STEP BACK OUT OF THE PICTURE FOR A MOMENT. OBSERVE THE SCENE WITHOUT JUDGEMENT. NOTICE THAT IS YOU IN THE PICTURE, GROWING AND LEARNING AND DOING THE BEST YOU CAN IN THAT MOMENT. THEN SAY TO YOURSELF SOMETHING LIKE, "HEY, IT LOOKS LIKE THE DECISION I MADE DID NOT GIVE ME THE RESULTS I EXPECTED", OR "BY GOSH, I CUT THAT BOARD TOO SHORT", OR "I GUESS I REALLY FEEL A LOT OF ANGER TOWARDS MY BOSS". THEN LOVE YOURSELF FOR THESE THINGS AND SAY SOMETHING LIKE, "OKAY NOW, THE NEXT DECISION WILL BE BETTER", OR "I WILL GET IT RIGHT THE NEXT TIME", OR "ITS OKAY THAT I FEEL THIS WAY". JUST LOVE YOURSELF!

IF YOU FIND IT DIFFICULT TO LOVE YOURSELF, THEN LOVE YOUR DIFFICULTY TO LOVE. LOVE YOUR DIFFICULTY TO FORGIVE, LOVE YOUR IMPERFECTIONS. YOU DO NOT CHANGE ANYTHING BY RESISTING, DENYING, OR HATING. YOU CHANGE EVERYTHING BY LOVING. LOVE YOUR NEGATIVE THOUGHTS AND YOU RELEASE YOURSELF FROM THEIR INFLUENCE. A LOVING THOUGHT IS MANY TIMES MORE POWERFUL THAN AN UNLOVING ONE. LOVE YOUR EMOTIONS BECAUSE YOU ARE HERE TO LEARN FROM THEM AND EXPERIENCE THEM. LOVE YOUR WEAKNESSES BECAUSE THEY SHOW YOU WHERE YOU NEED TO GROW AND DEVELOP. LOVE YOURSELF AND YOU RIDE THE GREAT CELESTIAL ESCALATOR TO ENLIGHTENMENT.

SUMMARY

LESSON 2

This lesson, and the practicing of it, has increased our awareness of what it means to love ourselves. We all have been taught that if we were not a certain way, according to society, then we were not okay. Therefore, each time we felt we had failed with this we had unloving feelings toward ourselves. Having done this over lifetimes, it is reasonable to say that it will take some time to turn it around. But as we began to practice loving everything about ourselves honestly, we did begin to notice some results.

Some of the results that we noticed were lighter feelings, our guilts lessening, our days going more smoothly, and just a better feeling toward life in general and toward ourselves. We are also learning that it is okay to feel certain feelings, and in so doing, we are able to let them go more quickly.

LESSON 3

I AM NOT THIS BODY - I AM A LIGHT OF GOD

THIS LESSON WILL INVOLVE LOOKING INTO A MIRROR - I CALL IT 'THE MIRROR EXERCISE'. TO BEGIN WITH, PLACE A MIRROR ON THE FLOOR AND THEN STAND OVER IT AND OBSERVE YOUR IMAGE. WHAT A FUNNY VIEW THIS IS! LAUGH AT YOUR REFLECTION AND SAY,"I AM NOT THIS BODY". THEN KNEEL DOWN CLOSER TO THE MIRROR AND AGAIN OBSERVE HOW FUNNY YOUR REFLECTION APPEARS. LAUGH AGAIN AND SAY, "I AM NOT THIS BODY". THEN GET DOWN REALLY CLOSE AND SEE YOUR REFLECTION. LAUGH AND SAY, "I AM NOT THIS BODY".

NOW THE LATTER PART OF THIS LESSON GOES AS FOLLOWS: EITHER SIT COMFORTABLY HOLDING A HAND MIRROR OR SIT IN FRONT OF A HANGING MIRROR. LOOK CLOSELY AT YOUR REFLECTION. STUDY YOUR FACE. NOTICE YOUR WRINKLES, YOUR PIMPLES, AND YOUR SCARS. IF YOU FIND YOURSELF JUDGING, LOVE YOURSELF

FOR IT AND LAUGH. YOU ARE NOT THIS BODY, YOU ARE MUCH MORE THAN THIS MASK OF FLESH AND HAIR WHICH LOOKS BACK AT YOU - YOU ARE A LIGHT OF GOD!

NOW CHOOSE EITHER YOUR RIGHT OR LEFT EYE AND GAZE INTENTLY INTO THE CENTER OF IT. ASK TO GET A GLIMPSE OF WHO YOU REALLY ARE AND SAY, "I AM NOT THIS BODY, I AM A LIGHT OF GOD". NOW AT SOME POINT, WHILE GAZING INTO THE CENTER OF YOUR EYE, YOU WILL NOTICE A BRIEF SHINY TWINKLE OF LIGHT. THIS IS THE REAL YOU LOOKING BACK, THE REAL YOU WITHOUT THE PHYSICAL MASK, THE IMPERFECTIONS, AND THE LIMITATIONS. THIS IS YOU, THE LIGHT OF GOD.

SOMETIMES PEOPLE IDENTIFY TOO STRONGLY WITH THEIR PHYSICAL SHELL, FORGETTING THAT THEY ARE SO VERY MUCH MORE. THIS IS ESPECIALLY TRUE WHEN THE BODY IS ILL, IN PAIN, TIRED, OR BEING JUDGED. SO WHENEVER YOU FIND YOURSELF TAKING YOUR PHYSICAL BODY TOO SERIOUSLY AND GETTING HUNG UP ON THE ILLUSION THAT IT IS WHO YOU ARE - REMEMBER THIS EXERCISE. YOU ARE NOT THIS BODY, YOU ARE A LIGHT OF GOD.

SUMMARY
LESSON 3

Using the mirror technique was quite an eye opener for us. We saw ourselves in ways we have never seen before. We saw every little zit and blackhead, every imperfection on our faces. It was downright scary! Because we were doing this exercise together, we had a lot of laughs, but on the inside we were really judging what we were seeing in that mirror.

Repeating the phrase, "I am not this body, I am a Light of God", really helped us to understand that we really were more than our imperfect faces were showing us. For most of our lives we were taught to believe we were our physical bodies and if they were not perfect, according to society, then neither were we. Inside though, we knew that there must be more to us than that and now Sonny had confirmed that for us.

We all had wonderful experiences and profound results looking into our eye and seeing the 'real self' that we really are. It brought about an inner knowingness that assured us we were more than our physical bodies. We use our mirror whenever we forget who we are and get stuck and bogged down with our physical selves. It helps us to remember who we really are.

LESSON 4

LIFE IS LIKE A RIVER

DO YOU FEEL LIKE YOU ARE STUCK AND NOT GOING ANYWHERE? DO YOU ALSO FEEL, SOMETIMES, THAT YOU ARE GOING IN TOO MANY DIRECTIONS AT ONCE AND NOT ACCOMPLISHING ANYTHING? DO YOU FEEL, SOMETIMES, LIKE THERE IS NOTHING HAPPENING IN YOUR LIFE?

TRY TO IMAGINE TIMES LIKE THESE AS RIVERS OF ENERGY. THERE ARE RIVERS WHICH CAUSE YOU TO FEEL NEGATIVE, STUCK, WORRIED, ANGRY, AND RIVERS WHICH ZAP YOUR ENERGY. THERE ARE ALSO RIVERS WHICH CAN MAKE YOU FEEL CREATIVE, FULL OF ENERGY, FULL OF JOY, AND RIVERS WHICH FILL YOU WITH SERENITY AND KNOWINGNESS.

LIFE IS LIKE A RIVER - FLOW WITH IT AND IT WILL TAKE YOU TO SOME WONDROUS PLACES. RESIST THE FLOW AND YOU TIRE YOURSELF WITH WASTED EFFORT.

WOULD YOU LIKE TO HAVE SOME FUN? I HAVE A WONDERFUL LITTLE EXERCISE FOR YOU THAT WILL HELP YOU TO BEGIN, ONCE AGAIN, TO FLOW ON THE RIVER OF LIFE. GET A BLANKET AND GO TO YOUR BACKYARD OR TO THE NEAREST GRASSY FIELD. LIE DOWN ON THE BLANKET, WITH YOUR HEAD AT THE CENTER. CLOSE YOUR EYES AND FIND YOURSELF ON A RIVER. NOTICE THE WATER. ARE YOU GENTLY FLOWING IN THE SMOOTH WATERS, OR ARE YOU IN A LOG JAM, OR IN A WHIRLPOOL, OR ON A SANDBAR, OR ARE YOU IN STAGNANT WATERS? WHERE ARE YOU ON THE RIVER OF LIFE? IF YOU ARE NOT FLOWING, THEN FIND A WAY TO REMOVE YOURSELF FROM THAT PLACE. MAKE A DECISION TO LET GO NOW AND FLOW ONCE AGAIN.

THIS EXERCISE WILL HELP YOU WHENEVER YOU FEEL THAT YOU ARE NOT IN THE FLOW. YOU WILL HAVE MORE ENERGY AND YOUR LIFE WILL RUN MORE SMOOTHLY. YOU WILL BE ABLE, ONCE AGAIN, TO MAKE DECISIONS AND YOUR LIFE WILL WORK BETTER FOR YOU. THE ENERGY THAT WAS USED TO RESIST THE FLOW WILL TRANSFORM AND BE USED TO CREATE A MORE POSITIVE LIFE FOR YOU.

HAVE FUN WITH THIS EXERCISE AND NOTICE AFTER YOU START FLOWING AGAIN HOW MUCH BETTER YOU FEEL AND HOW MUCH MORE POSITIVE YOU ARE.

SUMMARY

LESSON 4

We all had fun with this lesson. It happened to be a warm, sunny evening the night Sonny presented this lesson to us. And it just so happens we have a grassy park behind our apartment, so after receiving the lesson, we decided to head out to the park with our blanket to do the lesson.

We found a fairly secluded spot and laid down on the blanket as Sonny suggested, with our heads in the middle. (Luckily there weren't many people around to see or disturb us.) Before we could start the meditation, we had to quiet ourselves down. We were all feeling like little children, laughing and wondering what people would think if they were to see us all lying there on the blanket in this strange position. It took awhile, but we were finally able to quiet ourselves enough to get into the meditation.

The meditation turned out to be very enlightening for us. It showed us exactly what was happening in our lives. We were all trapped somewhere. Our experiences were all unique and we saw clearly where we were all trapped. The different ways in which we removed ourselves from these traps proved to be unique as well.

Angels reached into the whirlpool where I was spinning around and around and lifted me out and put me in an inner tube where I was then able to float peacefully down the river. Pat was helped by dolphins after her rubber raft was punctured. She was in a panic, splashing around trying to keep her head above water. The dolphins helped her find smooth water and she began to float down the river easily. Bess discovered that the log jam she was in was merely paper. She was able to break free easily and start flowing happily down the river. Chris was in turbulent water which pushed him into rocks, logs, and other debris floating around in the water. In order to free himself, he just started to relax and quit struggling. As he felt more in control, he was able to turn himself around and find more peaceful waters in which to flow.

We have found that this meditation works quickly, and it is uncanny how it lets us know what is happening when we aren't flowing with our lives.

LESSON 5

LETTING GO OF THE PAST IS LIKE TAKING OFF A HEAVY LOAD OF JUNK

YOU MAY HAVE HEARD THE OLD SAYING , "WHEN YOU LET GO OF THE PAST YOU MAKE ROOM FOR THE FUTURE". WELL, IT IS TRUE. WHEN YOUR MIND IS CLUTTERED WITH PAST ISSUES, EXPERIENCES, AND THOUGHTS, THERE IS LITTLE ROOM LEFT OVER FOR THE NEW TO COME IN.

IT IS TIME TO CLEAN HOUSE. IT IS TIME TO START TO CLEAR AWAY THE OLD. GO THROUGH YOUR HOUSE, YOUR CLOSETS, YOUR DRAWERS, UNDER YOUR BED, THE GARAGE, THE ATTIC, EVEN GO DOWN TO THE BASEMENT AND BEGIN SORTING THROUGH ALL YOUR OLD STUFF. SELL OR GIVE AWAY ALL THE USELESS JUNK THAT YOU NO LONGER IDENTIFY WITH. ALL THIS OLD STUFF JUST WEIGHS YOU DOWN WITH PAST MEMORIES THAT ARE NO LONGER ABOUT WHO YOU ARE OR WHO YOU ARE BECOMING.

DO THIS LOVINGLY AND AS YOU DO ASK YOURSELF, "HAVE I USED THIS LATELY?" "DOES IT SERVE ME ANYMORE IN MY NEW IMAGE?" THEN START TOSSING. NOTICE HOW LIGHT YOU BEGIN TO FEEL AS YOU CLEAR OUT THE PAST AND MAKE SPACE FOR THE WONDERFUL NEW FUTURE. REMEMBER THAT CLEARING OUT YOUR PHYSICAL SPACE ALSO CLEARS OUT YOUR CLUTTERED MIND.

I WOULD LIKE TO ADD FOR THOSE OF YOU WHO SOMEDAY MIGHT WANT A NEW RELATIONSHIP IN YOUR LIFE - OLD STUFF FROM A PAST RELATIONSHIP ACTS AS BARRIER TO KEEP SOMEONE NEW FROM COMING INTO YOUR LIFE. ONE DOOR MUST CLOSE BEFORE ANOTHER OPENS. SO LET GO GENTLY, LOVE AGAIN, AND LET YOURSELF BE LOVED.

SUMMARY

LESSON 5

At first we had a lot of resistance to doing this lesson, it sounded like work to us. But if you have ever really cleaned house and thrown away useless junk, you will recall the feeling it gave you. Not only the sense of accomplishment and satisfaction, but a light orderly feeling. We knew the rewards that this would give us, but still it sounded like quite a task. We had made a commitment to Sonny to do these lessons and we were determined to keep that promise. But still it didn't sound like fun. Pat had another concern which troubled her about the lesson. She wasn't really sure if she could part with her deceased husband's things. Sonny reassured her in this way. "*I WOULD NEVER LEAD YOU TO SACRIFICE. LET GO ONLY OF WHAT YOU CAN.*"

We procrastinated just a little, but we eventually did the lesson. We found it was easier than we expected and it gave us all great feelings of accomplishment. It affected our mental attitudes, as well as our physical environments. Chris experienced the feeling of taking off a back pack after carrying it around for too long. It proved to be more fun than we thought. It is like cleaning the cobwebs out of your windows and head at the same time.

We recommend this 'house cleaning' on a regular basis. It really does free you up and is very good therapy.

LESSON 6

DEALING WITH PROCRASTINATION

NOW THAT WE HAVE DEALT WITH THE PAST, WE WILL MOVE RIGHT ALONG AND DEAL WITH PROCRASTINATION. YOU KNOW ALL OF THOSE THINGS YOU HAVE BEEN PUTTING OFF - THOSE THINGS THAT KEEP YOU AWAKE AT NIGHT AND WILL NOT LET YOU RELAX. YOU KNOW THAT THEY WILL NOT LEAVE YOU ALONE UNTIL YOU DO THEM. YOU ARE NOT FREE TO GROW WHEN YOUR MIND IS BOGGED DOWN WITH ALL THAT YOU HAVE BEEN PUTTING OFF.

SO I WOULD LIKE YOU TO MAKE A LIST OF ALL THOSE THINGS THAT YOU HAVE BEEN PUTTING OFF. DECIDE NOW TO TAKE CARE OF ALL UNFINISHED BUSINESS. WRITE THOSE LETTERS, MAKE THOSE CALLS, FINISH UP ALL OF THOSE TASKS THAT YOU HAVE BEEN PUTTING OFF AND LETTING BUILD UP. THIS WILL REALLY SET YOU FREE

FROM OLD BURDENS AND PROMISES TO YOURSELF AND TO OTHERS.

GET ON WITH IT AND DO NOT FORGET TO FLOW WITH IT. SEE EACH TASK GENTLY FLOAT AWAY FROM YOUR PATH AS YOU JOYFULLY UNDERTAKE TO JUST DO IT - NO QUESTIONS ASKED! AS YOU COMPLETE EACH TASK, CROSS IT OFF YOUR LIST AND NOTICE HOW GREAT IT FEELS.

REMEMBER NOT TO LOOK UPON THIS LESSON AS A CHORE, BUT RATHER AS AN OPPORTUNITY FOR GREATER FREEDOM AND ACCELERATED GROWTH.

HAVE FUN DOING THIS AND WATCH HOW MUCH LIGHTER YOU FEEL AS THESE TASKS ARE CROSSED OFF YOUR LIST AND COMPLETED.

SUMMARY

LESSON 6

This one is a goodie! All of us procrastinate on a regular basis. We always have excuses. We are too tired, or we can think of better things to do, or we don't have time, or we really just don't want to do it. But we all knew, without even thinking about it, what we needed to put on our lists. It was as if Sonny was giving us permission to take the time and get these things out of the way. So we all decided not to procrastinate with them any longer. As we finished the tasks and crossed them off our list, we felt a great release and our guilt about them disappeared. We were finally able to say, "There I did it!"

We recommend doing this lesson on a regular basis, too. Give yourself that permission so that you can have all of those wonderful feelings that come after you are finished.

LESSON 7

HIGHER LOVE AND TAKING IT TO THE PEOPLE

IT IS TIME TO TAKE THESE LESSONS TO THE PEOPLE - LITERALLY! THE GREATEST GIFT YOU CAN GIVE IS THE LOVE IN YOUR HEART. LESSON SEVEN VERY MUCH INVOLVES TAKING YOUR LOVE TO THE PEOPLE. DECIDE WHERE YOU WOULD LIKE TO GIVE YOUR LOVE. IT CAN BE ANYWHERE WHERE PEOPLE MIGHT FEEL ISOLATED, UNLOVED, LONELY, SCARED, OR JUST IN NEED OF A FRIEND TO TALK TO. IT MIGHT BE WITH THE HOMELESS. IT MIGHT BE IN A NURSING HOME, OR IN A HOSPITAL. IT COULD BE WITH SOMEONE WHO IS SHUT-IN AND CANNOT LEAVE THEIR HOME. OR IT COULD BE ANYWHERE YOU MIGHT FEEL SOMEONE MIGHT BENEFIT FROM YOUR LOVE. DECIDE WHO YOU WOULD LIKE TO SHARE YOUR LOVE WITH. IT MIGHT EVEN BE A FAMILY MEMBER WHO WOULD APPRECIATE YOUR LOVE AND UNDERSTANDING.

IF YOU CHOOSE A HOMELESS PERSON, FOR INSTANCE, BUY THEM A MEAL OR PERHAPS A DRINK, BUT MOST IMPORTANTLY, LET THEM TALK AND REALLY LISTEN TO WHAT THEY ARE SAYING. SEE THE LIGHT OF GOD THAT THEY ARE. THIS IS A TRUE LESSON ON BECOMING THE TEACHER OF GOD THAT YOU ARE TRAINING TO BE. WRITE ABOUT YOUR EXPERIENCE. WHAT DID YOU LEARN ABOUT THEM AND YOURSELF? WHAT DID YOU LEARN ABOUT LOVE?

SUMMARY

LESSON 7

We, as a group, decided that we would go downtown and pick one of the homeless people. So the very next day we rode the train down to that section of town. It was just a matter of a few minutes before we found him. He appeared in a doorway less than a block away. We all knew that he was the one.

He was the first to speak. We all held our hands out to him to shake and introduced ourselves. He hesitantly held his out to us and said, as he took each of our hands, "You don't mind shaking this dirty old hand?" We assured him that we did not mind at all. With a smile on his face, he said back to us, "I guess one hand washes the other."

We all sat down on the street beside him. He seemed a little perplexed by our friendliness. We noticed, as we sat down, that he had a bottle of malt liquor deep within his ragged, dirt stained jacket. We could tell that he was feeling poorly as his hand shook when he reached into his jacket to find his bottle. He was very honest as he explained to us that not only was he homeless, but an alcoholic as well. We realized that he was too sick to go to a restaurant with us, so we offered to go and bring him back some food. He was very appreciative of our kindness.

As we sat and listened to his stories, we felt a tremendous amount of love in our hearts. He told us over and over again how much he enjoyed talking to us. He said that he talks to himself a lot because not many people will talk to him and he gets very lonely.

While he talked of his life, we felt the pain and the sadness that he carried around inside of him. He grew up in the midwest and then spent many years in the army. While in Germany, he met and married his wife. They had eight daughters together. Not long after their last child was born, his wife died in his arms of leukemia. Shortly after that, he was called to Vietnam. Four of his brothers died in that war and now he feels guilty that they died and he is still alive. After the war, he worked in rodeos and in the logging business so that he could educate his daughters. He seemed proud of the fact that he was able to do that for them. He kept telling us that he did not care about himself, only them. As he talked about his life and the people he loved, the tears flowed from his sad, bloodshot eyes. He touched each of us very deeply.

We also laughed with him and he sang songs to us. He told us that Hank Williams was his cousin and that they used to sing together.

We discovered that he sleeps under one of the bridges in town. He said the shelters in town were too wild for him - too many fights, so he doesn't go to them anymore.

Later we were visited by his brother who also lives on the streets. He had been watching us for some time and was curious as to who we were. It wasn't long before he started to trust us and began to tell us about his life. He told us how he had come from the streets and put himself through college. He told us he had degrees in both writing and drug and alcohol counseling. He did not tell us, however, what happened after that to put him back on the streets. He told us about a story he had written about life on the streets. It was about what success means to those on the streets. To those living on the streets, success means just making it through each day. If they are able to do that then they consider the day successful.

We learned so much from both of them. It was a day we shall never forget. We learned about ourselves, love, understanding, and compassion. We truly saw the Light of God that they are. They have left an impression on our lives that will last forever. We felt honored that they trusted us enough to share their lives with four complete strangers.

As we got up to leave, we held our hands out to each of them. They shook our hands and told us how we had made their day and how much it meant to them that we stopped to visit. If they only knew that they had made our day a most unforgettable one too!

On our next session with Sonny, he had this to say to us: "*YOU TOOK SO EASILY TO LESSON SEVEN. I AM SO PROUD OF MY FRIENDS. YOU ARE TRUE TEACHERS OF GOD. I CHOSE WELL WITH YOU AS MY MESSENGERS. PERHAPS YOU MADE THAT OLD MAN'S LAST DAYS MOST MEMORABLE. YOU LEFT HIM HAPPY AND AT PEACE. YOU GAVE HIM THE LOVE HE NEEDED. YOU DID A GREAT SERVICE TO ONE OF GOD'S CHILDREN.*"

LESSON 8

WHO ARE YOU?

LESSON EIGHT WILL INVOLVE IMAGE AGAIN. IT WILL INVOLVE TAKING A LOOK AT YOURSELF FROM OTHER PEOPLE'S POINT OF VIEW, AND ALSO LOOKING AT YOURSELF FROM A LIGHT AND POSITIVE POINT OF VIEW. YOU SEEM TO FORGET SOMETIMES JUST HOW MUCH OF A DIFFERENCE ONE OF YOUR SMILES COULD MAKE IN ANOTHER'S LIFE. YOU FORGET ALSO, HOW HEALING IT IS FOR YOU WHEN YOU LAUGH AND ARE HAVING FUN. IT IS VERY IMPORTANT FOR YOU TO DEVELOP A POSITIVE SELF IMAGE. SO THIS LESSON WILL HAVE YOU LOOKING AT YOUR SELF-IMAGE FROM BOTH POINTS OF VIEW.

LET US BEGIN WITH REALIZING HOW VALUABLE YOU ARE TO OTHERS. YOU CAN OFFER SO MUCH TO OTHERS BY BEING JUST WHO YOU ARE. BUT WHO ARE YOU? TAKE SOME TIME TO HONESTLY TAKE INVENTORY OF ALL THAT YOU MEAN TO THE PEOPLE IN YOUR LIFE. DO THIS FROM THEIR POINT OF VIEW - NOT YOURS. WHAT ROLES DO YOU PLAY IN THEIR LIVES? HOW DO THEY SEE YOU? HOW HAVE

YOU MADE A DIFFERENCE IN THEIR LIVES? YOU SOMETIMES THINK YOUR LIFE MATTERS NOT, BUT I TELL YOU, IT TRULY DOES. DO THIS FROM THAT PLACE WHERE YOU ARE THE 'LIGHT OF GOD'. SEE THE BIG PICTURE MADE UP OF EVEN THE SMALLEST WORDS OR SMILES.

THIS PART OF THE LESSON WILL GIVE THE MOST TROUBLE TO THOSE WHO HAVE DIFFICULTY SEEING THEIR OWN VALUE. IT MIGHT WORK BEST IF YOU WOULD FOCUS ON YOURSELF BEING THOSE OTHER PEOPLE. ACT OUT THEIR DAILY ROLES MENTALLY, THEN GENTLY TURN YOUR ATTENTION, AS THOSE OTHER PEOPLE, ON YOURSELF. WHAT ARE THEY THINKING AND FEELING AS THEY THINK ABOUT YOU? REALIZE THAT YOU ALWAYS HAVE THE POWER TO MAKE A DIFFERENCE IN PEOPLE'S LIVES. IT TAKES SO LITTLE AND CAN MEAN SO MUCH.

NOW FOR THE SECOND PART OF THIS LESSON. HAVE YOU EVER SAID TO SOMEONE, "TAKE A PICTURE, IT LASTS LONGER"? WELL, IT MIGHT INTEREST YOU TO KNOW THAT PHOTO BOOTHS WERE JUST MADE FOR PEOPLE LIKE YOU TO HAVE FUN IN.

IT IS TIME TO TAKE A FIELD TRIP TO THE NEAREST PHOTO BOOTH, DEPOSIT YOUR DOLLAR, AND TAKE FOUR WONDERFUL PICTURES OF YOURSELF. TAKE ONE OF YOU SMILING, ONE OF YOU LAUGHING, A SILLY ONE, AND A CORNY, CRAZY ONE. REALLY STUDY THOSE FACES THAT SHOW YOU HAVING FUN. THEY SAY SO MUCH. THEY CAN BE MOST HELPFUL AS A GROWTH TOOL FOR DEVELOPING YOUR POSITIVE SELF-IMAGE. THE TIME YOU SPEND IN LAUGHTER WILL WASH AWAY MANY HOURS OF PAIN AND UNHAPPINESS, FOR IT IS WRITTEN, "ONE WHO IS FILLED WITH HAPPINESS HAS NO ROOM FOR SADNESS." ALSO, "THEY WHO LAUGH FREELY EXPERIENCE GOD WITH EVERY CHUCKLE."

SO LAUGH OFTEN AT YOUR PHOTOS, KEEP IT LIGHT AND FUN. KEEP YOUR PHOTOS WITH YOU ALWAYS AND WHENEVER YOU NEED TO LAUGH, TAKE THEM OUT AND REMEMBER THE ABOVE SAYINGS. LOVE YOUR CRAZINESS, YOUR DESIRE TO GROW, YOUR NATURE, YOUR FRIENDSHIPS, YOUR ANGELS, AND YOUR GOD.

SUMMARY

LESSON 8

We all resisted doing the first part of this lesson. We put it off for a number of reasons; we weren't sure how to go about it, we were having trouble realizing our value to others, and it seemed like such a foreign thing to do. We weren't really sure how people felt about us and I think we were all a little afraid to find out. Sonny pushed us along, though, and told us that he would not give us the next lesson until we completed this one.

So we all got together to figure out what was hanging us up. We decided the best way to do it was to write letters to ourselves from these people. It worked! We found that the letters all flowed beautifully. It was as if those other people were actually writing the letters. We wrote all of our letters, and even wrote one to ourselves from God. When we were finished with this, we were able to see our value to others more clearly. We realized just how important we were to other people. It was a wonderful feeling!

Now the photo booth was great fun. We all went together to the nearest shopping mall and found a photo booth. We took turns getting our pictures taken. We laughed until we were all crying, as each set of photos popped out of the machine. Our photos were hysterical. People in the mall would walk by and stare at us strangely, which made us laugh even more.

Whenever we take ourselves too seriously now, we just take out our crazy photos and instantly our seriousness turns to laughter. It's magic! After we returned from the mall with our photos, we asked Sonny if he could see them. "*THE PHOTO EXPERIENCE WAS FUN, I PRESUME, FROM ALL OF YOUR LAUGHTER THERE. I CANNOT SEE THEM IN THE WAY THAT YOU DO, HAVING NO PHYSICAL EYES. I AM ABLE TO DERIVE INFORMATION AND FEELING FROM CONNECTING WITH AND OBSERVING YOUR ENERGIES.*"

LESSON 9

WRITING A DIFFICULT-TO-LOVE LETTER

LESSON NINE MAY BE A STRETCH FOR YOU, BUT VERY IMPORTANT FOR YOUR GROWTH AS TEACHERS OF GOD. IT IS EASY FOR YOU TO WRITE LOVE LETTERS TO ONES YOU LOVE. LESSON NINE WILL HAVE YOU WRITING LOVE LETTERS TO ALL OF THOSE YOU HAVE FOUND DIFFICULT TO LOVE. THESE LETTERS YOU WILL NOT SEND.

WHEN DOING THIS LESSON, GO AS FAR BACK AS YOU FIND NECESSARY. THE TEST WILL BE IF YOU CAN EASILY WRITE THE LETTER. IF YOU CAN, THEN YOU HAVE PROBABLY ALREADY HEALED THE SITUATION. IF IT IS DIFFICULT, I BELIEVE YOU HAVE SOME WORK TO DO.

IN THESE LETTERS INCLUDE AT LEAST FIVE NICE THINGS ABOUT THEM. THE NICE THINGS THAT WOULD COUNT ARE THINGS ABOUT THEIR CHARACTERS. CERTAINLY, THEY MUST HAVE SHOWN THEIR LIGHTS A FEW TIMES.

SEARCH FOR THESE TIMES. REMEMBER THAT THEY ARE LIGHTS OF GOD, TOO.

THIS WILL RELEASE YOU FROM ALL THE OLD GARBAGE YOU MAY STILL CARRY AROUND WITH YOU ABOUT THEM. YOU WILL HAVE HEALED YOURSELF OF PAST WOUNDS. DO NOT WOUND YOURSELF OR THEM FURTHER.

TAKE THE LETTERS AND READ THEM OVER UNTIL YOU ARE MOST COMFORTABLE WITH INCLUDING THEM ON YOUR LIST OF 'SPECIAL PEOPLE I HAVE KNOWN'. AND THEN CATCH NOT YOURSELF TALKING ILL OF THEM ANYMORE. THIS WILL EVOLVE YOU RAPIDLY, WHEN DONE HONESTLY FROM THAT PLACE WHERE YOU ARE THE LIGHT OF GOD.

SUMMARY

LESSON 9

Another tough one! This lesson gave us all a mixture of different feelings. We weren't sure we were ready to forgive everyone quite yet. There were those we were ready to forgive, but there were others who brought up resistance in us. With some we really had to search our minds and hearts to find the five nice character traits. This lesson wasn't as easy as it sounded.

The hardest part for me was getting to a place within myself where I could honestly move some of the people over to the 'Special People I Have Known' list. There is still one with whom I am struggling, but I am working on it. When you are able to do it though, it helps you to understand the other people better and to see them and the situations in a whole different light. You can see where they need to love themselves more and it also helps you have more compassion and understanding of where they are in their growth.

A wonderful surprise came out of this for Pat. She had written one of her letters to an old boyfriend of many years ago who had hurt her. After putting him over to 'The Special People' list, she started thinking and wondering about him and where he might be living now. We looked in the Portland phone book and sure enough, we found a listing. After some heavy prompting, Pat finally put her fears aside and called the number. He answered and he and Pat talked for a long time. Their friendship has resumed once again. This all came about because of this lesson, and of course as Sonny says, "*THERE ARE NO ACCIDENTS.*" You just never know what can result from doing this lesson.

It is a wonderful feeling to finally forgive and to let go of old resentments. Even though it may seem hard at first to write the letters, know that the benefits are worth all the work you may have to put into them.

LESSON 10

FIRST DECIDE WHAT YOU WANT

I REALIZE THAT PEOPLE SOMETIMES HAVE TROUBLE WHEN LISTENING FOR THEIR GUIDANCE. IT IS MOST IMPORTANT TO FIRST DECIDE WHAT YOU WANT, AND THEN ASK FOR GUIDANCE. DECIDING MUST COME FIRST, OTHERWISE NONE OF YOUR GUIDES KNOW WHAT TO HELP YOU WITH. THEY WILL NEVER SAY, "DO THIS OR THAT NEXT", UNLESS YOU SAY, " HEY, THIS IS WHAT I HAVE DECIDED I WANT, WILL YOU PLEASE GUIDE ME NOW?" SO YOUR LESSON IS TO DECIDE ON SOMETHING YOU WANT, ASK FOR GUIDANCE, AND LISTEN TO IT AND THEN FOLLOW IT.

BEFORE YOU ASK FOR GUIDANCE, IT IS MOST BENEFICIAL TO FIRST FIND THAT PLACE WITHIN YOURSELF WHERE YOU FEEL CONNECTED TO YOUR GOD SELF. FROM THIS PLACE, BE MOST SINCERE IN WHAT YOU WANT AND WHY YOU WANT IT. THEN LET GO OF ANY PRECONCEIVED IDEAS OF HOW YOU THINK THINGS WILL COME ABOUT.

BEGIN THEN TO BE GRATEFUL FOR HAVING ALREADY RECEIVED WHAT YOU HAVE ASKED FOR. THINK ABOUT HOW IT FEELS TO HAVE IT.

SOMETIMES WHAT YOU ASK FOR MAY NOT BE IN YOUR BEST INTEREST, AND YOU WILL BE TOLD THAT SOMEHOW. AGAIN LISTEN TO YOUR GUIDANCE AND SEE IF IT SUPPORTS WHAT YOU HAVE ASKED FOR.

PICK SOMETHING SIMPLE AT FIRST AND AFTER YOUR TRUST BUILDS, CHOOSE SOMETHING BIGGER. YOU WILL ALWAYS RECEIVE GUIDANCE, SO BE LISTENING INTENTLY AND BE ALERT. YOU MAY WANT TO LIST YOUR GUIDANCE DAILY IN REGARDS TO YOUR REQUESTS, BUT REMEMBER TO KEEP IT FUN.

SUMMARY

LESSON 10

We all had some trouble with this lesson. We knew we all wanted to create money, but listening for the guidance was where the problem came in. We had trouble distinguishing between wishful thinking and true guidance. Some of the voices we would hear were, "Just sit back and trust that it will come," or "Watch for a big miracle." We didn't know if we were to take steps to create it on our own, or just sit back until we were sure that what we were receiving was true guidance. It was confusing. We were all getting frustrated because our creations weren't manifesting. Also, we had ignored the part of the lesson which said to start out with something simple first. We wanted lots of money! So we decided to ask Sonny why we were having so much trouble. "*LET ME BEGIN BY WARNING YOU THAT MY WORDS AND MEANINGS CAN BE MOST ILL UNDERSTOOD AND CAUSE UNNEEDED GRIEF AND SEEMING BREACH OF TRUST. LET ME START OUT BY BEING VERY CLEAR WITH YOU ABOUT TRUST AND MIRACLES. FIRST OF ALL, AND PERHAPS MOST IMPORTANT, IS THE FACT THAT IN ORDER TO RECEIVE ANY KIND OF DIVINE GUIDANCE OR ASSISTANCE, YOU MUST KNOW WHAT YOU WANT, ASK FOR THE HELP, AND LISTEN TO GUIDANCE AFTER, I REPEAT, AFTER YOU YOURSELF HAVE DONE SOMETHING TOWARDS THAT DIRECTION. YES, THE VERY OLD SAYING IS TRUE, "GOD HELPS THOSE WHO HELP THEMSELVES." IT TAKES PRACTICE TO BECOME A SUCCESSFUL MIRACLE WORKER. IN OTHER WORDS, TAKE CARE OF YOURSELVES IN THE WAY WHICH YOU ARE ACCUSTOMED TO WHILE YOU PRACTICE MIRACLES, UNTIL YOU ARE READY TO LIVE THE WAY OF MIRACLES*". What Sonny said made sense to us, so we started to really look at our belief systems around money. We realized that some of them definitely had to be changed. We were not ready to create such large sums.

Another thing we had to look at with this lesson was: What did we really want to create in our lives? We knew that we couldn't just sit around and say, "Hey, what should I do next in my life?" We had to decide. It brought us to the understanding that we had to make the choices concerning our lives, instead of expecting our Angels and guides to do it for us. It put the responsibility on us.

We finally decided that large sums of money had to wait until we were able to change some of our old beliefs about money. So we all picked something simpler and we were all eventually successful. Guidance is still sometimes a problem, but we are getting much better at distinguishing true guidance from the rest of the garbage. We are even able to create small sums of money now.

LESSON 11

ADVANCED LISTENING

THIS NEXT LESSON WILL HELP YOU LEARN TO LISTEN BETTER TO THE GUIDANCE YOU RECEIVE. YOU ARE ALWAYS RECEIVING GUIDANCE, BUT RARELY DO YOU LISTEN. LESSON ELEVEN WILL HELP YOU BECOME AWARE OF YOUR LISTENING SKILLS.

DO YOU REALLY LISTEN TO OTHERS IN BODY ANY BETTER THAN THOSE IN SPIRIT FORM? I WANT YOU TO REALLY THINK ABOUT THAT QUESTION AND ANSWER IT HONESTLY. DO YOU REALLY PAY ATTENTION, OR DO YOU HAVE SO MUCH YOU FEEL YOU NEED TO SAY, OR THINK ABOUT, OR WORRY ABOUT, THAT YOU REALLY DO NOT HEAR OTHERS ?

I WANT YOU TO BECOME AWARE OF HOW WELL YOU LISTEN. THE NEXT TIME YOU HAVE A CONVERSATION WITH SOMEONE, SUSPEND FOR A MOMENT YOUR AGENDA, AND REALLY LISTEN TO WHAT THE OTHER PERSON IS SAYING.

YOU MAY BE MOST PLEASANTLY SURPRISED AT WHAT YOU HEAR.

GUIDANCE COMES TO YOU IN MANY WAYS, AND ONE OF THOSE WAYS IS THROUGH OTHER PEOPLE. WHEN YOUR MIND IS RACING WITH YOUR OWN THOUGHTS, IT IS VERY DIFFICULT TO HEAR ALL THAT IS BEING SAID TO YOU. IF YOU ARE HAVING TROUBLE HEARING YOUR GUIDANCE, IT CAN BE EXPLAINED WHEN YOU LOOK AT HOW WELL YOU LISTEN, OR RATHER LISTEN NOT, TO OTHERS. SO MAKE A SPECIAL EFFORT TO REALLY LISTEN EACH TIME YOU HAVE A CONVERSATION WITH SOMEONE.

THE MORE PROFICIENT YOU BECOME AT LISTENING TO OTHERS, THE MORE PROFICIENT YOU WILL BECOME AT LISTENING TO INNER GUIDANCE. REMEMBER EVERYONE AND EVERYTHING CAN BE THE VEHICLE THAT DELIVERS YOUR GUIDANCE. WHAT YOU HEAR JUST MIGHT WELL BLOW YOUR SOCKS OFF!

SUMMARY

LESSON 11

This lesson was really beneficial in helping us to understand guidance. We all had to admit that sometimes we did not really listen to others. We were too busy thinking our own thoughts and we missed half of what was being said to us. It takes practice to be a good listener. It takes practice to turn off our own thoughts and really focus on what someone else is saying. This lesson makes you aware of all the chatter that goes on in your mind when someone is talking to you.

When we were able to turn off our own thoughts, and really listen to others, we found truly amazing results. Answers or guidance came to us through others. We also found that guidance came to us through the radio, television, newspapers, and whatever else caught our attention.

We are not perfect listeners, by any means, but we are able now to catch ourselves when we aren't really listening to someone. It does take a lot of practice, though, to change our old listening habits.

LESSON 12

CREATING HEAVENLY DAYS AND NIGHTS

HOW OFTEN DO YOU START YOUR DAY GRUMBLING ABOUT HAVING TO GET UP AND GO TO WORK? THEN YOU STUMBLE THROUGH THE DAY JUST WANTING IT TO GET OVER, ONLY TO FIGHT RUSH HOUR TRAFFIC. YOU GET HOME AND HOPEFULLY FIND SOMETHING IN THE FRIDGE TO EAT, THEN YOU VEG OUT IN FRONT OF THE TUBE UNTIL YOU STUMBLE OFF TO BED. AND IN BED, YOU CANNOT SLEEP, EVEN THOUGH YOU ARE DOG TIRED, BECAUSE YOU ARE WORRIED ABOUT TOMORROW OR THE BILLS, OR THIS COMING UP, OR THAT WHICH YOU HAVE BEEN PUTTING OFF. DOES THIS SOUND FAMILIAR?

MAYBE YOUR LIFE IS NOT QUITE AS BAD AS THAT, BUT WOULD YOU SAY IT IS HEAVENLY? NOBODY IS GOING TO CHANGE THINGS FOR YOU. BUT I HAVE A SIMPLE LITTLE EXERCISE FOR YOU THAT WILL, IF DONE EACH DAY, GIVE

YOU HEAVENLY DAYS AND NIGHTS. ONLY YOU CAN CHANGE YOUR LIFE, FOR ONLY YOU HAVE THE POWER.

YOU START THESE LITTLE EXERCISES THE NIGHT BEFORE YOU WANT TO HAVE A HEAVENLY DAY. WHEN YOU FEEL YOU'VE HAD ENOUGH, TAKE FIVE LITTLE MINUTES - (IS THAT TOO MUCH TO ASK FOR TWENTY-FOUR GREATLY IMPROVED HOURS? I THINK IT IS A BARGAIN). IN THESE FIVE LITTLE MINUTES, YOU FIRST GO OVER YOUR DAY. WHATEVER YOU ARE NOT ABLE TO DO ANYTHING ABOUT, PUT INSIDE A WONDERFUL LITTLE ROCKET SHIP. AFTER YOU HAVE UNLOADED ALL OF YOUR BURDENS OF THE DAY, COUNT DOWN FROM TEN TO ZERO AND BLAST THE LITTLE ROCKET SHIP OFF INTO SPACE. THE THINGS THAT ARE SOMETHING TO REALLY BE DEALT WITH, YOU CAN TAKE CARE OF AFTER YOU HAVE HAD A GOOD NIGHT'S SLEEP, (WHICH IS REALLY THE PURPOSE OF A BED AND NIGHT). THEN TELL YOURSELF YOU WILL SLEEP SOUNDLY AND AWAKEN RESTED AND HAPPY TO START THE DAY, KNOWING IT WILL BE A MARVELLOUS DAY. TELL YOURSELF THE DAY WILL GO SMOOTHLY, PEOPLE WILL BE FRIENDLY, YOU WILL BE HAPPY AND THINK PLEASANT THOUGHTS, AND THERE WILL BE LOTS OF GOOD THINGS OUT THERE TO LOOK FOR. GIVE YOURSELF A LITTLE PICK-UP SESSION DURING THE DAY IF YOU FEEL YOURSELF SLIPPING BACK INTO THE OLD MODE. AT FIRST YOU MAY RESIST ALL OF THIS BECAUSE YOU ARE TAKING CHARGE OF YOUR LIFE AND ELIMINATING ALL THE THINGS YOU LOVE TO COMPLAIN ABOUT. BUT AFTER AWHILE, WHEN YOU START EXPERIENCING HEAVENLY DAYS AND NIGHTS, YOU WILL WONDER HOW YOU EVER GOT BY THE OLD WAY.

SUMMARY

LESSON 12

This lesson is fantastic! It worked for all of us the very first time and works every time we do it. The only time it doesn't work is when we don't do it.

Chris resisted a little at first because he was afraid he wouldn't have anything to complain about if he did it. But now when he does it, he has a much better day at work. Pat was having trouble falling asleep at night, but since she has been doing this lesson, she has not had one sleepless night. This exercise is great and the pick up session works quickly, too.

We all have our own little techniques of doing this lesson. Pat puts all her worries and cares on little playing cards with arms and feet and then demands that they march themselves into the rocket ship on their own. Chris pulls clumps of gunk off of his body and throws them into the rocket ship. Bess and I both use paper that we write our worries and cares on and toss them in. However you want to do it, works.

It really makes a difference in how well you sleep and what kind of day you have the next day. Like I said, the only time it doesn't work is when you don't do it. This exercise is wonderful!!

LESSON 13

I AM NOT THIS BODY, HOWEVER, I AM IT'S CARETAKER

THIS LESSON WILL INVOLVE USING YOUR MIRROR AGAIN. PLEASE HOLD THE MIRROR IN YOUR HANDS. LOOK AT YOUR FACE AND SAY, "I AM NOT THIS BODY, HOWEVER, I AM IT'S CARETAKER." THEN GET IN TOUCH WITH YOURSELF AS A LIGHT OF GOD. PRETEND THAT YOU ARE ONLY SPIRIT AND THE FACE IN THE MIRROR IS YOUR BODY. GIVE YOUR BODY A VOICE LIKE A SILENT VENTRILOQUIST. ASK BODY THINGS LIKE, HOW IS IT, WHAT DOES IT NEED, WHAT CAN YOU DO FOR IT. THEN LISTEN TO IT'S REPLY. IT MAY SAY FOR EXAMPLE: "THAT HEAT REALLY BOTHERS ME." "I NEED MORE VITAMIN A, LESS STRESS, MORE SLEEP, AND I NEED MORE HUGS. AND I HAVE BEEN HUNGRY FOR SOME PINEAPPLE AND MAYBE I COULD LOSE A FEW POUNDS OR LIGHT UP A FEW LESS CIGARETTES." BE GENTLE AND

LOVING WITH BODY AS YOU TELL IT HOW YOU ARE GOING TO BEGIN TO MEET IT'S NEEDS, MAKE IT'S LIFE MORE PLEASANT AND HEALTHY, AND LISTEN TO WHAT IT HAS TO SAY MORE OFTEN.

TO INCREASE YOUR LISTENING SKILLS, PLEASE PRACTICE THIS OFTEN. PRACTICE BOTH WHEN USING THE MIRROR AND ANYTIME, ANYWHERE, WITHOUT IT. THE RESULTS CANNOT HELP BUT BRING YOU INTO A MORE HARMONIOUS PLACE.

WHEN YOU BECOME VERY GOOD AT COMMUNICATING WITH YOUR BODY, YOU CAN ASK IT MANY QUESTIONS, SUCH AS: "WHAT SHALL I DO TODAY?", "WHAT SHALL I EAT?", "WHAT WOULD FEEL GOOD TO WEAR?", "WHERE SHALL I MOVE?", AND "WHERE WOULD I LIKE TO WORK?"

KEEP PRACTICING AND YOU WILL GAIN MORE CERTAINTY AND ELIMINATE DOUBT AND CONFUSION.

SUMMARY

LESSON 13

Sonny had us do this lesson right after we received it from him. We were amazed at how quickly our bodies responded to our questions. They didn't hesitate to tell us exactly what they wanted from us.

We wrote all of their requests down on paper so that we could see them in black and white. Some of the requests were easy enough to grant, but others were more difficult. We each have one or two that we are still procrastinating on. Some of us are procrastinating on losing a few pounds and some of us are having trouble cutting down on our cigarettes. We seem to find many reasons 'why not'.

We do know from this exercise what our bodies would like us to do for them - no question about it! Many of their requests are easier and we have been successful with them. I am sure, though, as we continue to grow and love ourselves more, that even those requests that seem hard now will become easier for us to do.

Sonny doesn't expect a 100% success rate with any of his lessons, as they are all ongoing lessons that will become easier and easier as we continue to grow.

Knowing that we are able to communicate with our bodies is a miracle and as we continue to take responsibility for our bodies' health, we will also be taking more responsibility for our spiritual growth. Don't be discouraged if you have trouble with some of your body's requests. Hang in there and do the best that you can.

LESSON 14

IF YOU CAN THINK OF IT, YOU CAN CREATE IT

THIS LESSON WILL HELP YOU TO CREATE. YOU WILL BEGIN FIRST BY CREATING SOMETHING SIMPLE, SUCH AS A FEATHER OR A COIN. CLOSE YOUR EYES AND THINK ABOUT YOUR OBJECT, HOLDING IT FIRMLY IN MIND. OBSERVE IT'S FEEL, TASTE AND SMELL, IF ANY. FOCUS ENTIRELY ON YOUR OBJECT UNTIL YOU CAN ALMOST FEEL THAT IF YOU OPENED YOUR EYES, IT WOULD BE THERE. DO THIS FIVE TIMES WITH FIVE SMALL OBJECTS. THEN DO THE SAME WITH FIVE LARGE OBJECTS, SUCH AS A RED VOLKSWAGON, A BEAR, OR A HIPPO.

SEE HOW LONG IT TAKES BEFORE YOU SEE OR HEAR ABOUT YOUR OBJECT. WHEN IT DOES APPEAR, MARVEL AT IT A MOMENT. WHEN YOU HAVE FINISHED CREATING YOUR TEN OBJECTS, DO THIS AGAIN WITH ANOTHER FIVE SMALL AND FIVE LARGE. THESE BEGINNER CREATIONS ARE NOT

MEANT TO BE FOR YOU PERSONALLY. AFTER ALL, WHAT WOULD YOU DO WITH A HIPPO? CHOOSE THINGS THAT YOU DO NOT REALLY WANT OR NEED.

AFTER YOU HAVE BEEN SUCCESSFUL WITH THESE TWENTY OBJECTS I WANT YOU TO PICK SOMETHING YOU REALLY WANT. CLOSE YOUR EYES AND VISUALIZE WHAT YOU WANT, BUT BE SURE TO PUT YOURSELF IN THE PICTURE. AGAIN FEEL IT, SMELL IT, TASTE IT, AND PRETEND YOU MOST CERTAINLY HAVE IT. WRITE A LETTER TO ME, TELLING ME HOW MUCH YOU ARE REALLY ENJOYING YOUR NEW CREATION. I AM ANXIOUS TO HEAR FROM YOU ABOUT YOUR NEW GIFT TO YOURSELF.

WHAT IS IMPORTANT TO REMEMBER IS THAT YOU CAN BRING THINGS INTO YOUR REALITY BY MEANS OF THOUGHT, IMAGINATION, AND FEELING. IT IS NO ACCIDENT!

SUMMARY

LESSON 14

This lesson proved to be successful for all of us. We had loads of fun watching and listening for all of our creations to show themselves. Sometimes they came to us in the strangest ways.

Bess was trying to create a turkey for Thanksgiving dinner. It was only a day or two after she did the exercise to create it, that her son brought a turkey home from his work place. She had completely forgotten that every year his company gave their employees turkeys for Thanksgiving. After receiving the turkey, she thought to herself, "Boy, that was easier than I thought it would be!"

This lesson really helped us to gain confidence in ourselves as creators. I think the secret to being successful with this lesson is not to try to create really outrageous creations until you get really good at creating the smaller ones. Building trust is the key here. The more you practice, the more trust you develop. This lesson really helps you understand how creation works. It has everything to do with our thoughts, imagination, and feelings.

LESSON 15

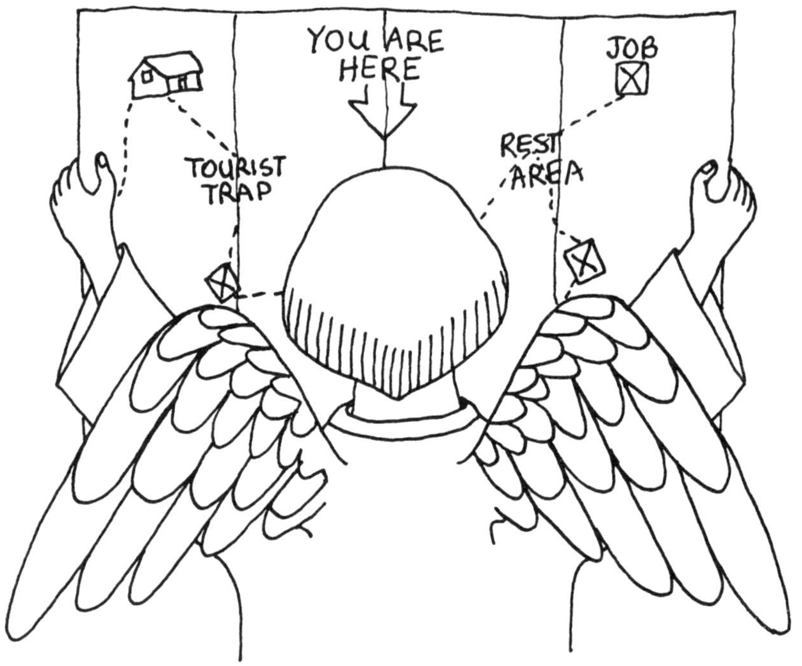

IF MY LIFE WAS A ROAD MAP, I COULD SEE WHERE ALL THE TOURIST TRAPS WERE AT A GLANCE

THE TIME HAS COME, MY FRIENDS, FOR ARTS AND CRAFTS. YES, WE WILL HAVE A LOT OF FUN MAPPING OUT OUR LIVES. THIS IS ANOTHER WAY TO HELP YOU CREATE THE THINGS YOU WANT IN YOUR LIFE.

PLEASE TAKE TWO SHEETS OF PAPER AND TAPE THEM TOGETHER - SIDE TO SIDE. TAKE ANOTHER PIECE OF PAPER AND MAKE A CUT-OUT WHICH SIGNIFIES YOU. IT IS BEST NOT TO MAKE YOUR CUT-OUT TOO HUGE, MAYBE FOUR INCHES HIGH. PUT THE CUT-OUT, THAT IS YOU, IN THE MIDDLE OF THE TWO TAPED SHEETS OF PAPER AND DRAW A SIGN THAT SAYS, "YOU ARE HERE."

THE LEFT SIDE OF THE PAPER WILL BE YOUR PAST. BEGIN ON THE RIGHT SIDE, YOUR FUTURE, AND SKETCH IN

A FEW SCENIC ROADSIDE STOPS THAT YOU WOULD LIKE TO VISIT - SUCH AS A GREAT NEW JOB, A RAISE, A LOVER, TRAVEL, MONEY, A BABY, BETTER HEALTH, PEACE OF MIND, OR A SPECIAL ACCOMPLISHMENT OR GOAL. DRAW LITTLE ROADS FROM WHERE YOU ARE IN THE MIDDLE TO EACH OF THESE.

NOW FOR THE FUN PART, FOR EACH OF YOUR SCENIC STOPS, DRAW A ROAD CONNECTING IT TO A TOURIST TRAP IN YOUR PAST WHICH WOULD SHOW A LOGICAL CONNECTION. FOR EXAMPLE, IF ONE OF YOUR SCENIC SIGHTS IS A TRIP - THEN CONNECT IT TO SOME TRIP IN YOUR PAST. IF YOU HAVE NEVER TRAVELED BEFORE, THEN MAKE SOMETHING UP. IF YOUR FUTURE SCENIC SIGHT IS A GREAT NEW JOB AND YOUR PAST EMPLOYMENT IS LESS THAN DESIRABLE, THEN CREATE A MEANINGFUL PAST JOB OR TWO THAT YOU CAN CONNECT IT TO.

THIS LESSON WILL HELP YOU TO VISUALIZE WHAT YOU WANT AND HELP YOU FOCUS ON WHAT IT IS YOU ARE TRYING TO CREATE. BE SURE TO KEEP IT LIGHT AND HAVE FUN. IF YOU ARE DOING THIS LESSON WITH OTHERS, SHARE YOUR MAPS WITH EACH OTHER.

SUMMARY

LESSON 15

The road maps were fun to do. We really had to think about everything we wanted to create in our lives and then figure out how they connected to our past. It took some brain work.

Chris is the only artist in the group and so his map was the only one that did not take a great deal of explanation to decipher. Our maps were creative - to say the least! We had a lot of laughs just trying to draw them! Each of us knew what we were drawing, but no one else had the slightest idea. And when it was time for us to explain them to the group, the others would laugh and say, "Oh, is that what it is?"

Some of our past experiences didn't make any logical progression to what we wanted in the future, so we had fun making things up. This is where you have the chance to be extremely creative with your imagination.

This lesson is really great, in helping you visualize what it is you are trying to create in your life. It is right there to look at and it helps program your subconscious mind. A good idea is to hang your map up where you see it whenever you pass by. Maybe you don't want to hang it where everyone who passes by will see it, unless, of course, you have great artistic ability. Otherwise you may have to spend a lot of time explaining what it is to people. This lesson helps reinforce to yourself what it is you want to create.

LESSON 16

MEETING YOUR GUARDIAN ANGEL

I AM GOING TO GIVE YOU A MOST MARVELLOUS MEDITATION, BUT FIRST I WOULD LIKE TO SHARE WITH YOU SOME OF THE FUNCTIONS GUARDIAN ANGELS PLAY IN PEOPLE'S LIVES.

WELL, BESIDES PROTECTION, THEY ALSO GUIDE INDIVIDUALS TO CERTAIN PEOPLE AND PLACES WHERE THEY THEN HAVE THE BEST CHANCE TO GROW AND LEARN THE LESSONS THEY CHOSE TO TACKLE THIS LIFETIME. GUARDIAN ANGELS COMFORT, HEAL, MAKE PEOPLE LAUGH, ADD SPICE TO ANY SOCIAL GATHERING, AND GENTLY PLAY IN PEOPLE'S DREAMS. THEY ALSO GIVE ENCOURAGEMENT AND LIGHT A FIRE UNDER YOU WHEN NEEDED. GUARDIAN ANGELS ALSO ASSIST INDIVIDUALS IN CONNECTING WITH THEIR HIGHER SELF, WHICH IS THE PART OF EACH PERSON THAT IS PLUGGED INTO GOD. A PERSON HAS BUT ONE

GUARDIAN ANGEL, HOWEVER, THERE ARE MANY ANGEL ASSISTANTS WHO WORK WITH THIS ONE.

NOW FOR THE MARVELLOUS MEDITATION. TO BEGIN WITH, LET US ASSUME YOU BELIEVE IN ANGELS AND HAVE AN OPEN MIND AND HEART. LET US ALSO ASSUME THAT YOU WANT TO MEET YOUR GUARDIAN ANGEL FOR THE PURPOSES OF SPIRITUAL GROWTH AND AWARENESS, NOT JUST FOR IDLE CURIOSITY. ASSUMING YOU MEET THIS CRITERIA, THEN LET US BEGIN BY GETTING VERY COMFORTABLE IN AN UPRIGHT POSITION. CLOSE YOUR EYES AND RELAX WITH WHATEVER METHOD WORKS BEST FOR YOU. NOW SINCE YOUR GUARDIAN ANGEL IS ALWAYS WITH YOU THERE IS NO NEED TO INVOKE OR CALL YOUR ANGEL IN. HE/SHE WILL MOST LIKELY BE STANDING RIGHT BEHIND YOU. ALLOW YOURSELF TO BECOME AWARE OF THIS PRESENCE. YOU MAY FEEL A WARMTH OR A TINGLING AS YOUR ANGEL PUTS HIS/HER HANDS ON YOUR SHOULDERS OR YOUR HEAD. FEEL THE LOVE. KNOW THAT YOUR GUARDIAN ANGEL IS HERE JUST FOR YOU - TO GUIDE, LOVE, AND HEAL YOU.

NOW IF YOU ARE READY, YOU CAN MEET YOUR GUARDIAN ANGEL FACE TO FACE. SENSE YOUR ANGEL COMING AROUND UNTIL HE/SHE IS SITTING OR STANDING RIGHT IN FRONT OF YOU. IF YOU KNOW YOUR ANGEL'S NAME, SAY HELLO. IF YOU DO NOT, THEN SAY HELLO AND ASK FOR THE NAME. YOU MAY HEAR IT, OR FEEL IT, OR KNOW IT, OR SEE IT. YOUR GUARDIAN ANGEL MAY APPEAR AS A LIGHT, OR A COLOR, OR IN HUMAN FORM, OR YOU MAY JUST FEEL A PRESENCE. NOTICE THAT YOUR GUARDIAN ANGEL IS HOLDING A LARGE GOLDEN BOWL OUT TO YOU. THIS IS THE BOWL OF TRANSMUTATION. IMAGINE ALL OF YOUR FEARS AND WORRIES, CONFUSION AND PROBLEMS, AS DARK, YUCKY GLOBS OF GARBAGE AND BEGIN TOSSING THEM INTO THE BOWL OF TRANSMUTATION. RELEASE EACH CHUNK OF DEBRIS WITH AN EXHALE. TEARS MAY ACCOMPANY YOUR RELEASE. WHEN YOU HAVE LET GO OF ALL THAT YOU ARE READY TO LET GO OF, YOU WILL FEEL MUCH LIGHTER AND FREER. THEN AS YOUR GUARDIAN ANGEL FOCUSES ENERGY ON THE BOWL OF TRANSMUTA-

TION FILLED WITH DEBRIS, IT BURSTS INTO FLAMES. AS THE FLAMES BURN HOTTER AND HOTTER, THE DEBRIS IS BEING TRANSFORMED INTO A HIGHER VIBRATION. WHEN THE FLAMES HAVE DIED DOWN, YOU WILL NOTICE A SMALL PILE OF GOLDEN DUST IN THE BOWL. THIS DUST CONTAINS SPARKLES OF INSIGHT, AWARENESS, IDEAS, SOLUTIONS, AND DIRECTIONS. YOUR GUARDIAN ANGEL TAKES THREE HANDFULS OF THE GOLDEN DUST AND TOSSES IT IN THE AIR OVER YOU. AS IT FALLS ON YOU, YOU HEAR A GENTLE TINKLING AS YOU FEEL IT PENETRATE YOUR BEING. YOU THEN NOTICE A TEAR OF JOY FORM IN THE CORNER OF YOUR ANGEL'S EYE. YOU WATCH AS IT CRYSTALIZES INTO A SHINY DIAMOND AS BRIGHT AS A STAR. YOUR ANGEL PICKS UP THE DIAMOND AND PLACES IT GENTLY ON YOUR HEAD AND GENTLY PRESSES IT IN THROUGH YOUR CROWN. THIS DIAMOND WILL ILLUMINATE YOUR MIND TO BETTER SEE THE NEXT STEPS YOU ARE TO TAKE. AS YOUR ANGEL MOVES AROUND BEHIND YOU ONCE AGAIN, KNOW THAT ANYTIME YOU NEED TO FEEL LOVED, NEED GUIDANCE, OR YOU WANT TO TRANSMUTE ENERGIES TO A HIGHER VIBRATION, THAT YOU CAN ALWAYS CALL UPON YOUR MARVELLOUS GUARDIAN ANGEL. WHEN YOU ARE READY, STRETCH, SMILE, AND OPEN YOUR EYES.

SUMMARY

LESSON 16

Meeting our own Guardian Angels and getting to know them has been a most profound experience for all of us. We were really excited when we learned what this lesson was about. Sonny had mentioned our Guardian Angels to us in previous sessions, so we were well aware that we had them, but now we were actually going to meet them face to face. We could hardly wait.

As the session began that evening, and before Sonny told us what the next lesson was to be about, he asked this question to Chris: "*WERE YOU GOING TO SHARE THE DREAM YOU HAD TODAY WITH THE OTHERS?*" Chris told Sonny that he hadn't planned on it, but that he would. Sonny then told Chris, "*IT WILL ALL BECOME MOST CLEAR TONIGHT.*"

Chris proceeded to tell us about his dream. His dream was very much like the meditation that Sonny gave us in this lesson. The sequence of events were almost identical, although the images in Chris' dream were slightly different than those in Sonny's meditation. For instance, Chris saw a yellow bucket instead of the golden bowl. The yucky globs of energy in the meditation were dirty potatoes in Chris' dream and the diamond was a shard of glass. Chris described the person bearing the yellow bucket as a young, beautiful woman with wings bigger than she was. She turned out to be Anola, Chris' Guardian Angel. We were all amazed, especially Chris, at how similar his dream was to the "Meet Your Guardian Angel" meditation Sonny gave us that evening.

We all had tremendous success with our first meeting with our Angels that night. We were all able to feel their touches, which was very exciting. Each one of us had some sense of what they were like.

Chris, of course, was able to see Anola clearly. I saw a male figure with blonde hair who appeared to be in his mid 20's. Bess sensed a male energy in front of her, which she described as expansive. Pat felt waves of love penetrate her being. She felt it was more a feminine energy rather than a masculine one. Our first experience with our Guardian Angels was rather breath-taking. When the meditation was over, we all felt so light and exhilarated. We felt as though a heaviness had been lifted from us.

Since then, we have all had numerous experiences with our Guardian Angels. Not only have we met them in subsequent meditations, but we have written them letters and also talked with them through the 'Angel Talk Board'. We have come to regard them as very intimate friends. Sonny calls them our gifts from God, which they certainly are!

Their personalities are really quite different. They do have one thing in common, however, and that is they do not beat around the bush if they have something to tell us.

Bess' Guardian Angel is Raphael, or Ropho for short. She describes him as a magnificent Angel who is likened to the power of a hawk and just as watchful. Raphael has had to light a fire under Bess a few times, but also gives her praise and encouragement as well. Raphael has a unique way with words. Here is an example of how he goes about lighting a fire under Bess. "*YO, BESS. ROPHO HERE. YES, AND NOW THAT I HAVE YOUR ATTENTION, CHILD, WE ARE GOING JOB FINDING. HELP ME OUT, DEAR, BY TRUSTING ME TO GUIDE YOU TO SOMETHING COOL. DO NOT SWEAT IT, HONEY, IT IS FOR YOUR GROWTH AND HIGHEST GOOD. DO NOT FIGHT ME, PLEASE. I AM YOUR LIFE-LONG BUDDY. I AM USED TO ALL YOUR TRICKS. REALIZE SOMETHING I GUIDE YOU TO WILL NOT BE SOMETHING TO SNIFF AT. LATER BABE.*"

Pat's Guardian Angel's name is Marshay; Buzz for short. Pat describes Marshay as sweet, caring, and giving. She is very gentle in dealing with Pat. Here is an example of Marshay's personality. (These comments came at a time when Pat's children were moving out on their own and she was ready to put her house up for sale.) "*THIS IS MARSHAY. HI PATRICIA, ARE YOU AS EXCITED AS ME ABOUT THE CHANGES COMING UP? IF NOT, WHY? I WILL HELP THE SITUATION. HOWEVER, AFTER YOUR HOUSE IS*

VACANT, THINGS WILL SPEED UP ON THEIR OWN. DO NOT OVERDO THINGS. IF YOU TRY TO HELP YOUR CHILDREN CARRY THINGS, I WILL CALL IN MISTER CHARLIE HORSE. PLEASE, PLEASE, PLEASE, TAKE CARE OF YOUR HEALTH - NO LIFTING, CARRYING, PUSHING, WORRYING, GUILT, AND NO STRESS! I LOVE YOU, DEAR ONE."

Chris' Angel, Anola, or Sunflower as the other Angels call her, is very gentle and wise and her messages are very much to the point. If Chris doesn't take her messages seriously or if he doesn't listen, Anola has a way about her that makes him take notice. She acts in a way that many females, trying to get a male's attention, might act. "*ANOLA HERE. GEE, CHRIS, YOU EITHER BELIEVE IN ME OR YOU DO NOT. I AM NOT A YO-YO. GIVE ME HALF A CHANCE TO WORK ON THINGS BEFORE YOU BLAST IT ALL, OK? CHRIS, I AM STILL WAITING FOR THOSE LONG WALKS YOU PROMISED ME, AND ANOTHER LETTER, BUT I LOVE YOU.*"

Booduin, or Boodie for short, is my Guardian Angel. He is very gentle with me, but does not hesitate to tell me when I need to be working on something. Here is an example of Booduin's personality. "*SUSAN, HI, I AM YOUR GUARDIAN, BOODIE. I AM SO PROUD OF YOU FOR CHANNELING YOUR NERVOUS ENERGY INTO TYPING THE LESSONS. BE CAREFUL NOT TO LET IT CONSUME YOU. TAKE TIME OFF TO EAT, WALK AROUND, AND HAVE SOME FUN. REMEMBER YOUR HEALTH, AND ABOVE ALL, DO NOT BE SO STUBBORN AS TO NOT LISTEN TO SUGGESTIONS AND CONSTRUCTIVE CRITICISM. YOU ARE MY SPECIAL ANGEL.*"

You may be wondering about the nicknames that our Guardian Angels have. It was during one of our sessions that Sonny told us about them. Here is what he said to us. "*MARSHAY, MARSHAY, DOTH BUZZ LIKE A BEE, SO THE NICKNAME BUZZ WAS GIVEN SHE. BOODUIN, BOODUIN WILL NEVER BE MOODY, WHEN YOU NEED A LAUGH JUST CALL HIM BOODIE. ROPHO, ROPHO, WHAT YOU WAIT FO'? ANOLA, ANOLA, HOLY GUACAMOLA. THEY LIKE A LITTLE PHRASE TO CALL THEM INTO ACTION.*" We have discovered they really do like it and they answer us much more quickly when we use our phrases.

As you can see, Guardian Angels are much more than protection for us. They are always willing to help us in any situation that will help us grow. They are there whenever we call on them, and of course even when we do not. They have been extremely helpful in answering any health question we might have. They have given us preventive measures to ensure our continuous good health. They have helped us understand parts of our lives that we didn't understand before.

Getting to know our Guardian Angels, and the other Angels who work with us, has been very exciting and has enriched our lives tremendously. We know that we will never have to face anything alone again!

LESSON 17

I GET BY WITH A LITTLE HELP FROM MY FRIENDS

THIS LESSON REQUIRES YOU TO SEE THAT THE ENTIRE WORLD, SEEN AND UNSEEN, IS MADE UP OF YOUR FRIENDS. THESE FRIENDS WANT FOR YOU EVERYTHING THAT YOU THINK WOULD MAKE YOU HAPPY, WITH THE HIGHEST GOOD FOR ALL CONCERNED. THEY ARE AT YOUR BECK AND CALL WHENEVER YOU NEED THEIR HELP IN BRINGING ABOUT THE RESULTS YOU DESIRE.

YOUR MISSION NOW IS TO PICK A WISH, ANY WISH YOU TRULY WANT, AND SIMPLY, BUT SPECIFICALLY, WRITE A LETTER DETAILING WHAT YOU WANT AND HOW EACH OF YOUR FRIENDS CAN HELP. WHEN WRITING THESE LETTERS, WRITE ESPECIALLY TO THOSE WHO WOULD BE DIRECTLY INVOLVED IN BRINGING YOUR WISH TO YOU. BUT DO NOT FORGET ANYONE, INCLUDING ANY AND ALL ANGELS.

BEGIN EACH LETTER WITH YOUR REQUEST AND END WITH GRATITUDE THAT THE WISH HAS BEEN GRANTED. SOMEWHERE IN THE LETTER, ASK THAT IT BE FOR THE HIGHEST GOOD OF ALL CONCERNED. SEAL EACH LETTER AND PUT THEM IN A SPECIAL PLACE, PREFERABLY NEAR YOUR BED. YOU CAN EVEN DRAW LITTLE ANGEL STAMPS ON THEM.

AFTER WRITING YOUR LETTERS, THINK ABOUT THEM GOING TO THE FRIENDS INTENDED. NOW COMES THE FUN PART. THE NEXT DAY PRETEND YOU ARE EACH OF THE FRIENDS THAT YOU SENT LETTERS TO. READ THE LETTER YOU RECEIVED, WITH LOVE. THEN WRITE A LETTER TO YOURSELF FROM EACH OF THEM, AS YOU WOULD WANT THEM TO WRITE IT, SAYING WHAT YOU WANT THEM TO SAY. YOU CAN EVEN SEND A NICE CARD. THESE LETTERS YOU WILL ADDRESS TO YOURSELF AND ACTUALLY *MAIL. IN A DAY OR TWO, YOU WILL GET LOTS OF MAIL FROM YOUR FRIENDS, SAYING VERY NICE THINGS AND TELLING YOU HOW MUCH THEY ARE GOING TO HELP YOU. THEY WILL TELL YOU HOW THEY ARE HELPING YOU TO HAVE WHAT YOU WANT EVEN AS YOU READ.*

IF YOU HAVE NOT RECEIVED THE RESULTS THAT YOU WANTED WHEN YOU EXPECTED, MAYBE IT WAS NOT FOR THE HIGHEST GOOD OF ALL CONCERNED. MEDITATE ON IT AND MAYBE SEND A FOLLOW-UP LETTER AND ANOTHER REPLY. HAVE FUN WITH THIS AND BE CREATIVE.

SUMMARY

LESSON 17

This lesson is one of our favorites. We have had so much fun writing the letters to our friends and especially to the Angels. An uncanny thing happens, though, when you receive your replies back in the mail. You read the letter and it feels as if what you are reading is a surprise to you. It is really strange in that respect. In fact, after you once seal the letter and put it in the mail, you immediately forget what you have written. We all had the same experience. We asked Sonny about it. "*I AM GLAD YOU ARE ENJOYING YOUR LETTER WRITING AND GETTING SUCH ANGELIC REPLIES. INTERESTING, IS IT NOT? IT ALWAYS WORKS. IT IS ACTUALLY THE ANGELS PREFERRED WAY OF TALKING TO PEOPLE. IT IS ACTUALLY THE ANGELS WRITING THE REPLIES, THROUGH YOU, OF COURSE.*"

We have had a couple of problems as well. The first one was that once in awhile we would receive a letter back from an Angel and it would give us wonderful predictions about our future which didn't happen. We would feel disappointed and confused. Sonny was able to give us some understanding and insight into why that would happen. "*I NEED TO EXPLAIN TO YOU THAT SOMETIMES WHEN YOU WRITE YOUR LETTERS TO ANGELS ABOUT AN EMOTIONALLY CHARGED ISSUE, THERE IS A CHANCE THAT YOUR NURTURING SELF STEPS IN WITH THE REPLY, INSTEAD OF THE ANGELS. ANGELS ANSWER EMOTIONALLY CHARGED ISSUES WITH LOVE AND GUIDANCE, INSTEAD OF WORDS. FOR BEST RESULTS IN COMMUNICATION, KEEP LETTERS LIGHT AND INTO THE NEUTRAL. REMEMBER IF YOU HAVE ASKED FOR SOMETHING AND HAVE NOT SEEN RESULTS YET, IT IS EITHER TAKING MORE TIME OR IT IS NOT FOR YOUR HIGHEST GOOD AT THIS TIME.*"

The other snag we had was understanding the phrase, 'For the highest good of all concerned.' We understood the obvious. We knew that if what we wanted would hurt someone, then it wasn't for the highest good of all concerned, but we wanted Sonny to explain it further. "*WHEN YOU EVOLVE TO THE POINT*

THAT YOU ARE NOW, YOU HAVE MANY TOOLS AT YOUR DISPOSAL FOR MANIFESTING YOUR DESIRES. ALL OF THESE INVOLVE CONSCIOUS CHOICE BASED ON WHAT YOU KNOW ABOUT WHAT YOU ARE ASKING FOR. WHEN YOU ENTER THE REALM OF ANGELS AND START ADDING THE PHRASE, "FOR THE HIGHEST GOOD OF ALL CONCERNED", YOU START PLAYING A NEW GAME WITH DIFFERENT RULES. WHEN YOU SAY THAT PHRASE, YOU PLACE YOUR DESIRE IN THE HANDS OF THE WISEST OF HEAVEN. THEY CAN SEE SO VERY CLEARLY HOW YOUR DESIRE WOULD AFFECT ALL THOSE CONCERNED. WHEN YOU SURRENDER YOUR WILL TO THE WISDOM OF HEAVEN, AND YOUR DESIRES TO THE WILL OF HEAVEN, THEN YOU MAY FIND THAT WHAT YOU WANTED IS NOT FOR THE HIGHEST GOOD OF ALL CONCERNED. THEN YOU WILL FIND THAT WE CANNOT HELP YOU BRING ABOUT YOUR DESIRE. IN FACT, WE WILL DO OUR DARNDEST TO STEER YOU IN ANOTHER DIRECTION. FURTHERMORE, THOSE OF YOU CONTEMPLATING A CHANGE IN EMPLOYMENT OR CAREERS, MAY MOST DEFINITELY WANT TO ASK TO BE GUIDED TO THAT SITUATION WHICH WOULD BE FOR THE HIGHEST GOOD OF ALL CONCERNED." Sonny also explained that we needed to take more time to think about our requests before we ask the Angels to help. This is how he explained it to us. "*CONFUCIUS ANGEL SAY: APPLE PIE BAKED FOR FIFTY MINUTES COMES OUT BETTER THAN ONE BAKED FOR EIGHT MINUTES. DOES THIS EXPLAIN MY VIEW ON LETTERS? IF YOU REALLY WANT SOMETHING, IS IT NOT WORTH SPENDING A LITTLE TIME ON IT? VERY PROFOUND, IS IT NOT?"*

We are getting better at recognizing these two snags, but it does take practice. We found that after writing two requests without any positive results, that we could usually look back and see that the Angels had given us signs that our request was not for the highest good of all concerned. But we had wanted our requests so much that we didn't want to acknowledge the signs.

The really wonderful thing about this lesson is the fact that you can write letters to your Guardian Angel and he/she will write back to you. We have all developed beautiful relationships with ours. After you have gotten to know your Guardian Angel, you will quickly be able to tell when it isn't your Angel writing to you. All Angels have their own distinct personalities.

Don't be discouraged if some of your requests fail. You will soon come to an understanding that those you called 'failures' turned out to be successes after all.

LESSON 18

TURN A CAUSE INTO APPLAUSE

YES, THIS IS SONNY'S 'ADOPT A CAUSE PROGRAM'. FOR THIS LESSON, CHOOSE A CAUSE THAT YOU REALLY BELIEVE IN AND THAT YOU CAN DO SOMETHING ABOUT. IT CAN BE THE HOMELESS, OR EDUCATION PROBLEMS, OR WHATEVER YOU CHOOSE. START A SCRAPBOOK OF ARTICLES, NOTES, MAIL, OR STORIES THAT PERTAIN TO YOUR CAUSE. THEN ASK FOR GUIDANCE AS TO WHAT YOU CAN DO TO HELP THE SITUATION. YOU CAN SEND SPECIAL ANGELS TO THE PEOPLE OR PLACES WHERE THEY CAN BE OF THE GREATEST GOOD TO ALL CONCERNED. MAYBE YOU CAN WRITE LETTERS, SPEAK TO PEOPLE, SEND MONEY, VOLUNTEER, OR DO SOME VISUALIZATIONS TO SEE THIS SITUATION IMPROVING. THEN START TO SEE OR HEAR THAT YOUR CAUSE IS MAKING IMPROVEMENTS. BELIEVING IS SEEING, NOT THE OTHER WAY AROUND.

YOU MAY WONDER WHAT THIS HAS TO DO WITH YOU AND YOUR GROWTH. EVERY SINGLE THING YOU DO, SAY, OR THINK, AFFECTS EVERYTHING ELSE IN THE UNIVERSE. *THIS IS ESPECIALLY TRUE WHEN YOU DIRECT ENERGY WITH A SPECIFIC INTENT TO A SPECIFIC THING. THERE IS NOT A CAUSE AROUND THAT YOU CANNOT INDIVIDUALLY OR COLLECTIVELY HAVE A POSITIVE IMPACT ON, IF YOU CHOOSE TO DO SO. SINCE EVERYTHING YOU CHANGE FOR THE BETTER AFFECTS YOU, THEN IS IT NOT EASY TO SEE HOW THIS LESSON CAN ONLY BENEFIT YOU AND THE REST OF GOD'S CHILDREN AS WELL?*

I WILL TELL YOU THIS, MY FRIENDS, THAT AFTER ONLY A VERY SHORT TIME OF GETTING OUTSIDE YOURSELF AND YOUR PROBLEMS, AND WHEN YOU START WORKING ON A CAUSE, YOU WILL DEFINITELY START TO NOTICE WONDERFUL CHANGES AND IMPROVEMENTS IN YOUR OWN LIFE. KNOW THAT EACH TIME YOU GIVE FROM THE HEART, YOU RECEIVE MANY TIMES BACK THE SAME, EVEN IF IT IS FROM ANOTHER SOURCE. NOTHING YOU GIVE IN THE NAME OF LOVE IS EVER LOST OR WASTED.

SUMMARY

LESSON 18

Bess, Pat, and I wanted to do something to help feed the hungry. We chose an organization in town that feeds hot meals to the elderly in our community. This organization prepares hot meals for those that are shut in for one reason or another, and also prepares hot meals for those who are able to get to the center. We decided to call and volunteer our time.

The experiences that we had, while volunteering, have been so rewarding. It is truly a wonderful feeling to know that we are helping to ensure that these wonderful Beings of Light have at least one hot meal a day. We interacted with those who came to the center and made many new friends. We worked very hard, but it didn't really feel like work because of the tremendous feeling of self-satisfaction and esteem that it brought us. While we were volunteering, we were able to get outside of our own issues and problems. We were able to use many of our previous lessons while doing this lesson.

Another thing we all did to help with this cause, was to send money to help feed the homeless. A thank you letter from this organization was then mailed to us. It helped show us that doing just a little can mean so much.

Chris wasn't able to volunteer at the center due to his work schedule, but he did do a number of meditations to help. He did choose to get involved with the recycling issue that is starting at his work place.

More recently though, we have all been working very hard to do what we can to help with world peace. There are many ways in which we are doing this - meditations, sending groups of Angels to help, and sending energies of love and peace to all of the areas of the world that need it.

We asked Sonny why is there so much dissension in our world. "*AS STATED PREVIOUSLY, WHAT GOD DID NOT MAKE DOES*

NOT EXIST. GOD SEES ONLY THE PERFECTION IN HIS CREATION. ALL ELSE IS ILLUSION AND SOME PEOPLE BELIEVE QUITE STRONGLY IN THEIR ILLUSIONS. CRIES OF "NO WAR!" ACTUALLY ADD CREDENCE TO THE ILLUSION. A BETTER ENERGY TO RADIATE IS PEACE AND OF COURSE, LOVE. AS PERSONAL CONFLICTS ARE HONESTLY LOOKED AT, FORGIVEN, AND RESOLVED AT HOME, SO WILL GLOBAL CONFLICTS FOLLOW. MANKIND DOES HAVE THE ABILITY TO CHANGE THE FUTURE. THE ANGELIC REALM IS GOING ALL OUT TO ASSIST THOSE WHO BELIEVE THIS TO BE SO ."

We have noticed getting involved in this cause has definitely taken the focus off of ourselves and we have realized how insignificant some of our 'so called problems' are. We highly recommend this lesson and hope you will see the importance of it.

LESSON 19

MAKING A LIST AND CHECKING IT TWICE.

TO DO THIS LESSON SUCCESSFULLY REQUIRES DILIGENCE, FORGIVENESS, AND A WHOLE HEAP OF HUMOR. HOW ABOUT A PILE OF HUMOR? HOW ABOUT A GREAT CAPACITY TO POKE FUN AT YOURSELF?

THE ABOVE MENTIONED LIST WILL CONTAIN, FOR ONE SOLID DAY, ALL OF THE NEGATIVE THOUGHTS YOU HAVE. EVERY TIME YOU CRITICISE YOURSELF OR ANOTHER, IT GOES ON THE LIST. EVERY FEAR OR JUDGEMENT YOU ENTERTAIN GOES ON THE LIST. PITY - THE LIST; FAILURE TO SEE THE HUMOR IN LIFE - THE LIST; LETTING THINGS BUG YOU - THE LIST; AND WORRY - THE LIST.

NOW FOR THE LIGHTER SIDE OF THE LESSON, WHOOPEE! THE PURPOSE HERE IS NOT TO SEE HOW NAUGHTY YOU HAVE BEEN. OH NO, YOU ALREADY KNOW THAT, RIGHT? AND, OF COURSE, YOU SEE THE WORST, AND

THEN YOU WOULD HAVE TO ADD THAT TO THE LIST ALSO. THE PURPOSE IS TO BEGIN TO CATCH YOURSELF IN THE ACT, THEN QUICKLY FORGIVE YOURSELF AND HAVE A HEARTY LAUGH ABOUT IT. BUT FOR THAT ONE DISGUSTING DAY, PLEASE MAKE A LIST. THEN THAT EVENING, BEFORE YOU RETIRE TO YOUR SLUMBER CHAMBER, READ THE LIST, FORGIVE YOURSELF ONCE MORE, AND HAVE SOME HILARIOUS LAUGHTER FOR A NIGHT CAP. I KNOW THAT YOU WILL REALLY ENJOY THIS ONE.

DID YOU THINK THAT WAS ALL FOR LESSON NINETEEN? NOOOO WAY, JOSE! YOU ARE BUT HALFWAY HOME. DAY TWO OF THE LIST EPISODE - THE SECOND DAY, AND IDEALLY FROM NOW ON, YOU WILL STILL BE CATCHING YOURSELF IN THE ACT, THEN FORGIVING YOURSELF AND LAUGHING. YOU WILL THEN RE-PROGRAM YOUR THOUGHTS BY IMMEDIATELY COUNTERACTING THE NEGATIVE THOUGHTS WITH POSITIVE ONES. THE MORE YOU DO THIS, THE BETTER YOU GET AND THE MORE FUN IT IS. MAKE A GAME OF IT. NO GAME SHOULD LEAVE YOU LESS THAN AMUSED!

SUMMARY

LESSON 19

This lesson proved to be very enlightening for all of us. It's amazing how many of our thoughts and feelings pass through us without our conscious awareness, that is until we really take the time to become aware of them. When doing this lesson you begin to monitor this and it can be somewhat frightening. Here we are trying to create positive realities for ourselves and at the same time letting our thoughts and feelings run rampant with negativity. It is no wonder we have trouble creating the realities we really want. As stated in a previous lesson, it is our thoughts, feelings, and imagination that create our reality. This lesson really helps us become aware of what we really think and feel.

Chris was startled that he had over 20 items on his list before 10:00 AM. After that, he started catching himself and was able to stop the thought or feeling before he let it take over.

Bess had a long list that first day also, but now is catching herself more often. She made up a little technique that she uses when she does catch herself. She places a white cloud above her head and puts all of the negative thoughts into this cloud and sends it off to God.

Pat had only a few on her list, claiming that it must have been one of her better days!

I, also, had only a few. I believe that I was on guard that day, knowing this was the day for the dreaded 'list'. The next day, however was a different story!

This lesson helped us become aware of our thoughts and feelings. We are not always successful, however, in catching ourselves. There are still times we seem to enjoy wallowing in our negativity. At these times, we have given each other permission to point this out. We are getting better now at recognizing when we are in one of those negative frames of mind. Changing our thoughts and feelings has made a big difference in how we see our lives and ourselves.

LESSON 20

HOW DO I LOVE THEE, LET ME COUNT THE WAYS

GOD IS CONSTANTLY SHOWING YOU HOW MUCH HE LOVES YOU. EVERY GOOD THING THAT EXISTS IS GOD'S GIFT FOR YOU TO ENJOY. THE MORE YOU NOTICE THESE GIFTS, THE MORE YOU EXPERIENCE HIS LOVE.

SPEND ONE DAY NOTICING GOD'S GIFTS. NOTICE THE TREES, MOUNTAINS, CLOUDS, THE SUN, THE MOON, PEOPLE, AND NOTICE YOUR BODY, YOUR SENSES, YOUR TALENTS, AND YOUR ANGELS. ARE THESE NOT THINGS TO BE MOST GRATEFUL FOR? YOU MAY OPT TO DO SOME SOUL SEARCHING TO HONESTLY TAKE STOCK OF THE GIFTS YOU HAVE NOT BEEN APPRECIATING. WHEN YOU APPRECIATE A GIFT, YOU TAKE GOOD CARE OF IT, YOU ENJOY IT, AND YOU USE IT FOR YOUR HIGHEST GOOD.

WHAT GIFTS ARE YOU ABUSING? WHAT GIFTS ARE YOU CRITICAL OF? WHAT GIFTS ARE YOU NOT USING TO THE FULLEST? DO NOT GET HEAVY WITH THIS, INSTEAD FORGIVE YOURSELF AND LAUGH. THEN MAKE A COMMITMENT AND ASK FOR HELP TO CHANGE THINGS IN THOSE AREAS.

YOU MAY FIND YOURSELF NOTICING GOD'S GIFTS WITH MORE APPRECIATION FOR THE REST OF YOUR LIFE. NOW IS THAT NOT A MOST WONDERFUL WAY OF SAYING THANK YOU TO GOD?

SUMMARY

LESSON 20

For this lesson we thought we would take a trip to the coast and observe all of God's gifts there. It was a beautiful day and we gathered early for our trip.

The drive down to the coast took 1 1/2 hours. Most of the way down, we were silent as we observed all the beautiful scenery along the way. Oregon is beautiful with all of it's greenery. We also saw many animals grazing in the fields. Mt. Hood was especially gorgeous that morning. We made a special effort to notice everything as we drove along. We looked at things as if we were seeing them for the first time. It was an incredible feeling.

After we arrived, the first thing we did was to go to the grocery store to buy six loaves of bread to feed to the seagulls on the beach. We found a little spot near a log to settle down to wait for the seagulls. It didn't take long for our little seagull friends to find us. It was quite an experience to get to know them all. They each had their own distinct personality. One in particular, just screamed at us so that we would notice him and feed him some bread. There were two that were brave enough to come right up to us and eat the bread right out of our hands. Others that were more timid and shy would just hover above us and wait for us to throw bread up at them. The sun was bright and as we looked up to them they looked like little Angels above us. It didn't take long before we were out of bread and Chris volunteered to go back to town for more. At one point, we had left the bread by the log to walk down to the water. The seagulls seized the opportunity and grabbed a loaf of bread and promptly tore it open. It was so much fun watching them.

The day was an extraordinary day for all of us. The Angels provided us with a fantastic light show in the sky. We all saw these beautiful flashes of different colored lights dancing across the sky. We were all very curious about this so we asked

Sonny if it had any special significance. This was his answer. "*IT WAS JUST A GIFT.*" Of course it was more than that to us!

Another really amazing and interesting thing happened that afternoon to Chris. We brought a bottle of champagne so that we could toast God and all of our Angels. Chris had drawn a picture of Sonny in the sand and while we were all heading toward the drawing, the cork started to twist on it's own, while in Chris' hand, and then it popped off. It landed right in the middle of Sonny's drawing. It startled Chris, to say the least! We then poured our glasses, and also poured some on Sonny's mouth. We watched it as it sank deeply into the sand. Sonny commented on it later that evening. "*I HAD SUCH A WONDERFUL SUNDAY. I HAVE NEVER BEFORE HAD CHAMPAGNE, AND OH, THE BIRDS! DID I SURPRISE YOU WITH MY CORK TRICK?*" Until this confirmation, we didn't know how to explain what had happened with the cork. Amazing things start to happen when you start working with the Angels!

This day contained many wonderful surprises and miracles. It gave us a feeling of oneness with God and the universe. We felt intense gratitude for the many gifts that God had given us. I doubt that we will ever take these gifts for granted again.

LESSON 21

LETTING YOUR GIFT GIVE YOU A LIFT

SOMETIMES WHEN YOU ARE FEELING DOWN, IT IS BECAUSE YOU HAVE NOT BEEN ABLE TO USE YOUR GIFTS. GOD'S GIFTS ARE POWERFUL. THEY CAN HEAL, THEY CAN RESTORE YOUR SENSE OF PURPOSE AND MEANING, AND BRING YOU GREAT JOY AND FULFILLMENT. GIFTS UNUSED CAN CAUSE PAIN, FRUSTRATION, DEPRESSION, ANGER, LACK OF FULFILLMENT, PURPOSE AND MEANING, AND EVEN DEATH.

COULD THE MAN WHO HIDES HIS GIFTS GIVE ANYTHING TO THE WORLD? NO! NEITHER CAN THE MAN WHO SPENDS HIS DAY TOILING AT WHAT HE LOVES NOT.

TAKE A DAY, JUST FOR YOU, TO USE ONE OR MORE OF YOUR GIFTS. GET TOTALLY IMMERSED IN IT. ALL YOU NEED TO DO TO BE HAPPY IS TO UTILIZE YOUR GIFTS AND TO REALLY PUT YOUR HEART INTO WHAT YOU DO. THEN WILL

HEAVEN BE NO IDLE FANTASY, BUT INDEED, A SHINING REALITY.

SO TAKE A DAY, JUST FOR YOU, AND BAKE A PIE, WRITE, SING, DANCE, PAINT, FISH, PLANT A GARDEN, BUILD SOMETHING, SWIM, MAKE CALLS, BUT CHOOSE A DAY, JUST FOR YOU, TO USE YOUR GIFTS. NOTICE HOW IT MAKES YOU FEEL. NOTICE HOW ALIVE YOU FEEL. NOTICE HOW TIME FLIES. BUT MOST OF ALL, HAVE FUN!

SUMMARY

LESSON 21

This was an exciting lesson, as we were given permission to take time off from our responsibilities to do what we really loved to do. The permission, of course, was not necessary, but sometimes we tend to put restrictions on ourselves by saying we just do not have the time to do what we love to do. There are many self-imposed reasons why we do not give ourselves permission. We forget just how important it is for our own well being to take the time to use the wonderful gifts God has given us.

Chris made his day extra special. He also decided to take a day off work to use his gift. Chris is an artist and used his day to paint a portrait of Sonny as he perceives him. It is a beautiful painting and hangs in our living room. Sonny was pleased and had this to say about his first portrait. *"SINCE CHRIS' MARVELLOUS PAINTING, THE WHOLE WORLD WILL KNOW THAT I AM A REDHEAD. THANK YOU FOR THE HONOR OF GRACING YOUR LIVING ROOM."*

Pat used her day to go to a local hospital and volunteer her time. Once every week now, she has the opportunity to use her special gift of healing.

I love to write, so I used my day to go to a nearby park where I could relax, feed the squirrels, and do some writing.

Bess' newly surfacing gift is her poetry. She used her day to write poems, which seemed to flow from her that day.

We knew the joy of using our gifts, but we also knew the frustration, depression, and the many other emotions Sonny described in this lesson when we don't use them. We have come to realize the importance, more than ever now, of using these gifts. We have concluded that we have to set time aside for this, just as we set aside time for other things in our lives. By doing so, we have discovered a new found energy that helps the other areas of our lives run more smoothly.

LESSON 22

***EXPERIENCE AND YEARN
TO GROW AND TO LEARN
NO MATTER WHAT,
STAY OUT OF A RUT***

WHEN WE ANGELS OBSERVE HUMANS, IT IF OFTEN WITH A GREAT DEAL OF CURIOSITY AND AMUSEMENT. WE ARE PARTICULARLY PUZZLED BY THE WAY YOU FALL SO EASILY INTO A MONOTONOUS DAILY ROUTINE. EVERY DAY, THE SAME OLD THING. THE SAME TIME FOR THIS OR THAT. THE SAME ROUTE TO WORK. THE SAME BREAKFAST, LUNCH, AND DINNER. SHOPPING AT THE SAME STORE FOR THE SAME THINGS. SATURDAY IS LAUNDRY DAY; SUNDAY NIGHT - FRIED CHICKEN; TUESDAY - BOWLING; FRIDAY NIGHT - GET A BABY-SITTER AND CATCH THE FISH AND CHIPS SPECIAL AT YOUR USUAL RESTAURANT. MONDAY - PAY THE BILLS; DO NOT FORGET THE PAPER BOY BECAUSE I GOTTA HAVE MY PAPER EVERY MORNING WITH MY COF-

FEE - MOUNTAIN GROWN, OF COURSE! BORING, BORING, BORING!

THOUGH THIS MAY SOUND A BIT EXTREME, CAN YOU NOT IDENTIFY YOURSELF TO SOME DEGREE IN THIS SCENARIO OF THE ULTIMATE RUT? WE ANGELS WONDER WHY YOU ALLOW YOURSELVES TO DEVELOP HABITS AND FIXED PRACTICES AND MONOTONOUS ROUTINES. DOES IT NOT MAKE LIFE VERY UNEXCITING AND DULL? PERHAPS THERE IS A FALSE SENSE OF SECURITY IN KNOWING WHAT TO LOOK FORWARD TO DAY AFTER DAY. PERHAPS YOU FEEL YOU ARE TOO TIRED TO THINK, TO LEARN, GROW, EXPERIENCE, EXPLORE, BE SPONTANEOUS, OR CHANGE. IS BEING IN A RUT ANY WAY TO LIVE YOUR LIFE? I DO NOT WISH TO IMPLY THAT ALL HABITUAL PRACTICES ARE CONTRARY TO YOUR LIFE'S PURPOSE. FAR FROM IT! KEEP BRUSHING YOUR TEETH, BATHING, AND USING DEODORANT, FOR PETE'S SAKE, BUT MAYBE TRY A NEW BRAND OF TOOTHPASTE, OR ADD SOMETHING TO ENHANCE YOUR BATH, OR TRY A NEW UNDERARM DEODORANT FROM A DIFFERENT STORE. AND DO SO CONSCIOUSLY, PLEASE. DO NOT SPACE OUT AND DEVELOP ANOTHER RUT.

THE DANGER OF BEING IN A RUT IS THAT YOU MISS OUT ON OPPORTUNITIES FOR GROWTH. YOU MISS OUT ON LIFE. AND BEFORE YOU KNOW IT, THE YEARS HAVE JUST WHIZZED BY AND YOU STRUGGLE TO TRY AND RECALL WHAT YOU REALLY GOT OUT OF IT ALL. WHEN YOUR PRESENT INCARNATION HAS REACHED IT'S CONCLUSION, AND YOU LOOK BACK ON IT AND SEE HOW YOU LIVED IT, HOW INTERESTING WILL IT BE? WILL YOU BE PROUD TO ANNOUNCE THAT YOU HAD YOUR CORN FLAKES EVERY MORNING FOR TEN YEARS? WAS YOUR LIFE'S PURPOSE FULFILLED WHEN YOU DIED ON THAT SPOT WHERE YOU PLOPPED DOWN EVERY NIGHT TO FALL ASLEEP IN FRONT OF THE TUBE? NO! YOU MAY WELL FIND, MUCH TO YOUR DISMAY, THAT IN REGARDS TO HOW FULLY YOU EXPERIENCED LIFE, YOU WERE DULL. KNOW THAT THE ONLY DIFFERENCE BETWEEN A RUT AND A GRAVE IS THE DEPTH.

SO HERE IS YOUR LESSON. IT WILL REQUIRE ONE WEEK TO DO. EACH DAY DO SOMETHING DIFFERENT TO CHANGE YOUR ROUTINE AND MAKE IT LESS OF A HABIT AND MORE FUN AND INTERESTING. TAKE A DIFFERENT ROUTE TO WORK; SHOP AT A DIFFERENT STORE; EAT A NEW VEGETABLE; ATTEND A WORKSHOP OR LECTURE ON AN INTERESTING TOPIC.

WHEN YOU GET OUT OF A RUT, THERE ARE MANY WONDERS AND SURPRISES TO BE FOUND. GROW, REACH, LEARN, EXPAND, EXPERIENCE, DISCOVER, AND STAY OUT OF A RUT. HAVE FUN!

SUMMARY

LESSON 22

This lesson was a lot of fun and made us look at the ruts we had gotten ourselves into. Doing this lesson helped us understand we were responsible for much of what we complained about.

Changing our routine just a little helps to make life much more interesting and exciting. It is like traveling to and visiting a new area that you aren't familiar with. It brings a new vitality to life that's not there when you are caught up in ruts and routines.

We have noticed though, that we have periods of getting back into the old ruts and routines, and have concluded that there must be some kind of security that we derive from it. Old habits are not always easy to break. But whenever we realize what we are doing, we quickly decide to get out of them, because it is much more fun and exciting to do so. Our boredom disappears and we get a new perspective on life.

LESSON 23

APPRECIATE ANOTHER PLACE, LOVING ALL THE HUMAN RACE

SOMETIMES YOU TEND TO GET STUCK IN YOUR LITTLE CORNER OF THE WORLD. YOU SOMETIMES FORGET THAT THERE ARE OTHERS, JUST LIKE YOU, WHO LIVE IN OTHER PARTS OF THE WORLD. THERE ARE OTHERS, LIKE YOU, WHO ARE WANTING TO GROW AND MAKE THEIR LIVES A LITTLE HAPPIER, MORE FULFILLING, PEACEFUL, AND THEY WANT TO FIND SOME KIND OF PURPOSE FOR THEIR EXISTENCE. THEY MAY NOT SPEAK THE SAME LANGUAGE AS YOU; THEY MAY NOT EAT THE SAME KIND OF FOOD THAT YOU DO; THEY MAY NOT EVEN LOOK ANYTHING LIKE YOU DO, OR HAVE THE SAME CUSTOMS. BUT THEY ARE ALL CONSCIOUS OF WANTING TO GROW AND STRETCH, AND THEY TOO ARE LIGHTS OF GOD.

I WANT YOU TO BECOME MORE AWARE OF THESE OTHER PEOPLE WHO SHARE YOUR PLANET. I WANT YOU TO

START TO REALIZE HOW MUCH LIKE YOU THEY REALLY ARE. THEY ALL FEEL PAIN, JOY, SADNESS, LOVE, ANGER, AND ALL OF THE VERY SAME EMOTIONS THAT YOU FEEL. THE ONLY REAL DIFFERENCE BETWEEN YOU IS THE AREA IN WHICH YOU WERE BORN.

SO I WANT YOU TO PLAN A DINNER PARTY. YOU MAY WANT TO INVITE OTHERS TO JOIN YOU, OR YOU MAY WANT TO PLAN A SPECIAL DINNER JUST FOR YOURSELF. I WANT YOU TO PICK A FOREIGN COUNTRY THAT YOU WILL STUDY. LEARN AT LEAST ONE INTERESTING CUSTOM OF THAT COUNTRY. THEN I WANT YOU TO LEARN TO WRITE AND SAY THESE FIVE WORDS IN THE LANGUAGE OF THAT COUNTRY: GOD, ANGEL, LOVE, JOY AND LAUGHTER. FOR YOUR DINNER, I WANT YOU TO PREPARE A NATIVE DISH FROM THAT COUNTRY.

HAVE FUN WITH THIS AND BEGIN, FROM NOW ON, TO SEE THE SIMILARITIES, RATHER THAN THE DIFFERENCES. REALIZE THEY ARE LIGHTS OF GOD, TOO.

SUMMARY

LESSON 23

We enjoyed this lesson immensely. We had so much fun doing the research and preparing the meal. We used the library and also a large bookstore here in Portland.

Bess, Pat, and I were lucky enough to talk to people from the country we had chosen. I chose Brazil, because earlier there had been a chance we might be transferred there by Chris' company. In Portland, we have a Brazilian restaurant where I had lunch and talked with the owner. He was kind enough to help me with the pronunciation of the Portuguese words I had found.

Bess chose France, because she feels a connection with this country and loves the romantic way the language sounds. As she was researching her words in the bookstore, she met some French students who helped her with the pronunciations.

Pat chose Japan, because she feels a love for the country and it's people. Pat was stumped as to how to pronounce the words, but one evening while playing bingo, she happened to sit across from two Japanese women who were more than willing to help her with this.

Chris chose India, because of his ongoing fascination with that country. He wasn't lucky enough to meet anyone from that country, but he did learn to write the words with perfection.

We planned a dinner party where we each prepared our foreign dishes. The food was quite interesting, to say the least! Our dishes were not like anything we have ever had in this country. As we sat around sharing our food, we also shared the customs we had researched about our countries.

We learned a lot from our dinner party that evening. As we ate their food, and discussed their customs we noticed that we felt a closeness with the countries we had chosen; and a oneness with their inhabitants. Doing this lesson makes this big world of ours seem a little smaller. We talked in detail of the similarities that people all over the world share. Like Sonny says, the only difference, rather the only real difference, we have, is the country in which we were born.

LESSON 24

SIGN, SIGN, EVERYWHERE A SIGN

I SAW A WET SIGN THE OTHER DAY, AND BEING WHO I AM, I TOUCHED IT ANYWAY. BUT IT WAS DRY. THE SIGN MAY HAVE BEEN CORRECT AT ONE TIME, BUT NOW IT WAS NO LONGER RELEVANT. IT WAS REFERRING TO A CONDITION OF THE PAST.

HOW MANY OUT-OF-DATE SIGNS DO YOU CONTINUE TO WEAR, SUCH AS, "I HAVE NO TALENTS"; "I HAVE NO MONEY, NO JOB, NO ENERGY, NO DIRECTION, POOR HEALTH, AND I AM UNHAPPY"?

IT IS TIME TO DO SOME SOUL-SEARCHING TO IDENTIFY YOUR OLD SIGNS. WRITE THEM DOWN ON LITTLE SCRAPS OF PAPER. THESE YOU WILL TAPE TO YOUR CLOTHING. IF YOU ARE DOING THIS LESSON WITH A GROUP, YOU WILL WEAR THESE SIGNS IN FRONT OF THE GROUP - LIKE IN A FASHION SHOW. IF YOU ARE DOING THIS LESSON ALONE,

GO OVER TO THE MIRROR AND LOOK AT YOURSELF WITH ALL OF THOSE OLD OUT-OF-DATE SIGNS. ONE AT A TIME, PLUCK EACH OLD SIGN OFF AND READ IT OUT LOUD AND THEN DISCARD IT.

NOW WRITE NEW SIGNS ON SOME PRETTY PAPER WHICH WILL REFLECT THE PRESENT YOU. THINGS LIKE; "I AM LOVABLE, HAPPY, ABUNDANT", ETC. TAPE THESE TO YOURSELF, ONE AT A TIME, WHILE STATING THEM ALOUD TO THE GROUP OR TO THE MIRROR. HANG THESE NEW SIGNS UP IN YOUR HOME AFTERWARDS. THEY WILL BE LIKE AFFIRMATIONS FOR YOU WHICH WILL HELP YOU REAFFIRM YOUR NEW BELIEFS, UNTIL THEY BECOME THE REALITY YOU WANT. HAVE FUN AND REMEMBER *YOUR NEW SIGNS.*

SUMMARY

LESSON 24

This lesson took some real soul-searching. We had to stop and think about what signs we carried that were no longer relevant to our growth and to who we were becoming. Most of them, we came to realize, were actually hindering what we were trying to create in our lives. Reciting and believing in those old signs gave contradictory messages to our subconscious minds and to our unseen friends who were trying to help us.

After we had each discovered these old signs, we got together to finish the lesson. We put a lot of energy into doing the lesson, especially Bess, who actually got into character to further illustrate her intention. She dressed up in tattered clothes and taped all her old signs onto her clothing. She even wore a mask of the grouch (that of Oscar from the television show *Sesame Street.*) On the way over to our apartment that evening, she stopped at a grocery store to pick up a bottle of champagne so that we could toast the ending of our old signs and the beginning of our new ones. While at the store, many people stopped and stared at her, which delighted her. She was enjoying this lesson to the fullest!

We had a great time ripping off these old signs, one by one, and affirming that we were done with each of them. After completing this part of the lesson, we further affirmed our intentions by burning them outside in our BBQ.

It was now time to write our new signs. After we had finished writing them, we noticed that Bess had disappeared. She had gone into the bathroom, where she took off her tattered clothes, and put on a very nice outfit, which symbolized her transformation. While in the bathroom, she noticed a bandana in her bag. She had never seen it prior to now and she was very puzzled by it. The bandana had a beautiful picture of a Pegasus on it, which we later discovered means 'poetic inspiration'. She came out wanting to know which one of us had given it to her. None of us had. It was a mystery to her because it had not been there prior to her leaving home. We asked Sonny about it later that evening. "*ROPHO LOVES YOU ENOUGH TO GIVE YOU A BANDANA FACTORY.*" Needless to say, Bess was, and still is, in awe that she was given a gift from her Guardian Angel! Astonishing things start to happen when Angels come into your life!

As to how we are doing with our new signs - all in all, quite well. But of course, there are times when our old signs do creep back in. At those times we realize that it is the old signs talking and we don't want to identify with them any longer. We realize that they can no longer be an excuse for us and we must dismiss them quickly. We are re-programing our thoughts, and we recognize that it doesn't happen overnight. We do get frustrated sometimes though when our physical reality doesn't reflect our new signs as quickly as we would like. But we understand that it takes time for reality to show us our new beliefs.

LESSON 25

FEED THE SPIRITUALLY HUNGRY

THERE COMES A TIME WHEN LESS FORTUNATE PEOPLE CAN SHOW US SO MUCH ABOUT WHAT WE ARE HERE TO LEARN AND DO. LESS FORTUNATE CAN MEAN THEY DO NOT HAVE THE RESOURCES FOR PERSONAL AND SPIRITUAL GROWTH. IF YOU COULD REMEMBER YOUR MISSION HERE, YOU WOULD BECOME AWARE THAT WE ALL NEED TO HAVE THAT CHANCE. IT IS FOR THE GOOD OF ALL CONCERNED.

LESSON TWENTY-FIVE IS TO FEED THE SPIRITUALLY HUNGRY. IT IS IMPORTANT, AS TEACHERS OF GOD, THAT WHEN YOUR CUP IS FULL, YOU SPILL IT ON THE HUNGRY SOULS OF YOUR FELLOW BEINGS HERE ON EARTH. IT IS EQUALLY IMPORTANT NOT TO POUR YOUR GUIDANCE AND WISDOM ON THE ONE WHOSE SOUL IS CLOSED. WATER FLOWS BEST INTO THIRSTY MOUTHS, OPEN HANDS, AND EMPTY CUPS.

SO PART OF THIS LESSON INVOLVES DEVELOPING THE INSIGHT TO KNOW WHEN ONE IS IN NEED OF YOUR GUIDANCE AND WISDOM, AND WHEN ONE IS NOT. YOU MAY, OF COURSE, ASK ME OR YOUR GUARDIAN ANGEL FOR ASSISTANCE. HAVE FUN!

SUMMARY

LESSON 25

We have all had success with this lesson. We have had many opportunities to engage in conversations with those who were spiritually hungry. We discovered something in doing this, and that is; what we end up conveying to them is something we need to reinforce within ourselves. The old saying, "We teach best what we need to learn," is true in many cases.

We have also come across many who could have used some spiritual guidance, but were unwilling to hear. It has been fairly easy to distinguish between those who are receptive and those who are not. This lesson involves using the 'Advanced Listening' lesson. By listening intently to the other person, you can usually tell if they would be open to any spiritual help from you. We have also run into those that we weren't sure of, so in those cases we just mentioned a little something to check out their response. If what we said was not heard, or was ignored, then we knew that at least we had planted a seed.

Bess has been extremely successful with this lesson. She has the opportunity to come in contact with many young people who come to her home to visit her son. She says for the most part, they are hungry for knowledge, and the opportunity to talk about such matters. She has had many enlightening discussions with these young people, and finds them eager to learn and very receptive.

On the whole, we have been very successful with this lesson. When we have been able to give, in that respect it has created wonderful feelings in us. We have a lot of enthusiasm for what we have learned from Sonny, and we seize every opportunity that presents itself to talk about what we have learned thus far. But we have to be careful not to intrude on someone's free will to believe as they wish. We will continue to plant seeds in those we feel may want to know more at a later date.

LESSON 26

THE QUALITIES OF BEING THERE ARE THE VEHICLES TO GET YOU THERE

LET US TAKE THE ISSUE OF MONEY. IS IT NOT REALLY WHAT MONEY WILL GIVE YOU THAT YOU WANT AND NOT THE MONEY ITSELF? REALLY LOOK AT THAT STATEMENT. IF YOU HAD MORE MONEY, WOULD YOU NOT BUY SOMETHING, OR PAY THE BILLS? AND WOULD DOING THAT NOT GIVE YOU MORE JOY, FREEDOM, PEACE, ALIVENESS, SELF ESTEEM, AND FULFILLMENT? SO IT IS ACTUALLY THESE HIGHER QUALITIES THAT YOU WANT. THEN I TELL YOU, THAT IF YOU FIRST DEVELOP THESE HIGHER QUALITIES IN YOU, THEN THEY WILL ATTRACT ABUNDANCE IN ALL THINGS. IF YOU HAVE NOT FIRST DEVELOPED THESE HIGHER QUALITIES, THEN THE MONEY MAY NOT GIVE YOU WHAT YOU WANT IT TO GIVE. THE MONEY MAY MAKE YOUR LIFE MORE HECTIC, INSTEAD OF BRINGING YOU PEACE OR

FREEDOM. THE UNIVERSE HAS NEVER SAID, "YOU MUST FIRST WIN THE LOTTERY BEFORE YOU CAN ENJOY THE HIGHER QUALITIES YOU WANT AND RICHLY DESERVE." THE WONDERFUL THING IS THAT YOU CAN START RIGHT NOW, AND IT COSTS YOU NOTHING - ZERO!

TO PLAY, YOU CAN TAKE A LOOK AND MAKE A LIST OF WHAT YOU WOULD DO IF YOU WON A LOT OF MONEY. THEN BOIL IT DOWN TO THE HIGHER QUALITIES YOU REALLY WANT. THEN FIND CREATIVE WAYS TO GIVE YOURSELF THESE FEELINGS. IN SHORT ORDER, YOU WILL START ATTRACTING ABUNDANCE LEFT AND RIGHT. WITH THESE HIGHER QUALITIES ALREADY WITHIN YOU, YOU WILL TRULY ENJOY YOUR ABUNDANCE, BECAUSE YOU HAVE ALREADY FILLED THOSE NEEDS AND WANTS YOU THOUGHT MONEY WOULD PROVIDE.

ASK YOUR GUARDIAN ANGEL TO HELP YOU GET IN TOUCH WITH THE HIGHER QUALITIES YOU TRULY WANT. MEDITATE IN SILENCE, HEAR THE WORDS IN YOUR HEART. IF YOU RESONATE TO THEM, THEN YOU HAVE THE CORRECT HIGHER QUALITIES IN WHICH TO DEVELOP. BE SURE TO WRITE THEM DOWN. THINK OF AS MANY WAYS AS YOU CAN TO GIVE THESE TO YOURSELF. THINK OF WHEN YOU FELT THOSE THINGS IN YOUR PAST. WHAT ELEMENTS WERE PRESENT WHICH CONTRIBUTED TO YOUR OVERALL EXPERIENCE OF THAT HIGHER QUALITY?

YOU MAY NOT WANT TO PROCRASTINATE WITH THIS LESSON. HAVE YOU NOT WAITED LONG ENOUGH TO KNOW THE HAPPINESS THAT AWAITS YOU - LIKE A WARM BLANKET ON A COLD NIGHT; LIKE A COOL BREEZE ON A MUGGY NIGHT; LIKE A COLD DRINK ON A DRY, PARCHED AFTERNOON; LIKE A RAINBOW AFTER THE STORM; AND LIKE DESSERT ANYTIME?!

TRANSFORMATION DOES NOT HAPPEN TO YOU. TRANSFORMATION TAKES PLACE WITHIN YOU AND RADIATES OUT FROM YOUR CENTER. THE SPEED IN WHICH A TRANSFORMATION TAKES PLACE IS DIRECTLY PROPORTIONATE TO THE DEDICATION IN THE 'TRANSFORMEE'.

SUMMARY

LESSON 26

Sonny had us do this lesson that same night. We took the issue of money, as he suggested, because it is something we all would like to have more of. It was interesting to discover what it was we were really wanting. Sonny was absolutely correct in that it was the higher qualities we hoped money would give us. We helped each other discover these higher qualities by sharing our own discoveries and by asking each other pertinent questions. When we weren't sure if we were correct, then we would ask our Guardian Angels to help us. We would then get a feeling inside that told us if we were correct. Some of the higher qualities we all agreed on were: freedom, peace of mind, joy, happiness, and security.

The next thing we did was search our minds and our pasts for situations and activities that had brought about those feelings before. We each found our own individual ones, but we also discovered that many of Sonny's previous lessons also brought these higher qualities to us 'Turn A Cause Into Applause'; 'Higher Love And Taking It To The People'; and 'Feed The Spiritually Hungry'. In fact, most of the prior lessons have brought about these higher qualities. And of course, whenever we feel connected with our Guardian Angels, we feel many higher qualities coming to the surface. Each of you will discover for yourself the specific lessons that will bring about these higher qualities in you.

We have not been 100% successful in developing these higher qualities on a consistent basis as of yet, but we are working on it, and we do know many ways in which to develop them. We have come to realize that it is not the 'things' we want, but what we thought they would provide for us.

LESSON 27

AS YOU LOVE IT, RISE ABOVE IT

HAVE YOU EVER NOTICED HOW YOU ARE STUCK WITH THOSE THINGS, PEOPLE, SITUATIONS, OR CONDITIONS YOU HATE, RESIST, DREAD, AND DESPISE? ONE OF THE SADDEST STUMBLING BLOCKS THAT TEACHERS OF GOD ENCOUNTER IS DIFFICULTY LOVING THE UNLOVABLE OR RATHER, WHAT YOU HAVE DECIDED IS UNLOVABLE. IF YOU WANT TO GET THAT CREEP OUT OF YOUR LIFE; GET OUT OF THAT DEAD-END JOB; GET OUT OF YOUR POVERTY; OR GET AWAY FROM YOUR STRUGGLING: THEN FIRST LEARN TO LOVE THEM OR IT. WHEN YOU REACT IN A NEGATIVE WAY TO PEOPLE, PLACES, AND THINGS, YOU DO SO FOR NUMEROUS REASONS. THE REASONS USUALLY BOIL DOWN TO ONE - YOUR LESSON WAS TO LOVE THEM SO YOU COULD MOVE ON TO OTHER LIFE LESSONS. WHEN YOU HAVE NOT GOT THE LESSON, OR YOU ARE HAVING A DREADFUL TIME

WITH IT, GUESS WHAT?, YOU ARE STUCK UNTIL YOU LEARN IT WELL ENOUGH TO MOVE ON.

DRAW FROM EARLIER LESSONS, WHERE YOU SEE THE LIGHT OF GOD IN THAT PERSON AND LOVE THEM AS THAT LIGHT. REALIZE YOUR VALUE TO OTHERS, OR WHAT THAT JOB HAS GIVEN YOU, AND LOVE IT. THEN GET ON DOWN THE ROAD!

ANY CONDITION - MENTAL, EMOTIONAL, OR SPIRITUAL - AS YOU LOVE IT, RISE ABOVE IT. IF YOU CANNOT LOVE SOMEONE DUE TO HIS BEING A REAL PAIN IN THE REAR, THEN LOVE THEM FOR GIVING YOU A CHANCE TO LEARN A LESSON AND EVOLVE. LOOK AT EVERYTHING IN THIS LIGHT. THEY ARE ALL GIVING YOU A CHANCE TO LEARN AND LOVE AND TO GROW. SO LOVE IT ALL, THEN YOU WILL HAVE LIFTED YOUR FINAL IMPEDIMENTS FROM YOUR PATH TO THE LIGHT!

SUMMARY

LESSON 27

This lesson is one we have to work consistently on. We understand the importance of rising above those situations and problems we deal with in our everyday life, but sometimes it is not as easy as it sounds. We have our days when we are able to do it and we find those days to go extremely well for us. But then we have those days when we find it almost impossible to feel any kind of love for our situations. Those days, we find, are much harder to get through. At times, we have gotten really frustrated and so we have called upon our Angels to help us with our lives. One evening, at a regular session, we thought that Sonny was going to give us another lesson, but instead he had this to say. "*WHEN WE ANGELS WATCH PEOPLE, WE SOMETIMES SHAKE OUR HEADS AND LAUGH. IMAGINE A PERSON IN A HOUSE SITTING ON A PILE OF BRAND NEW TOOLS. THE ROOF LEAKS, THE WALLS NEED PAINTING, LIGHT BULBS NEED REPLACING, THE DOOR WILL NOT CLOSE, AND THE WINDOWS ARE STUCK CLOSED. DAY AFTER DAY, THIS PERSON BEMOANS THE SITUATION. "WOE IS ME, I AM VERY UNHAPPY IN THIS SITUATION. I HAVE ASKED FOR HELP, BUT NONE CAME. OH, WHEN WILL THOSE ANGELS COME TO FIX MY HOUSE? HOW LONG MUST I WAIT FOR THINGS TO CHANGE?" IS THIS PERSON SILLY FOR SITTING ON ALL THOSE TOOLS, INSTEAD OF USING THEM TO FIX THE HOUSE AND CREATE A HAPPY SITUATION? ARE YOU NOT SILLY IF YOU DO NOT USE THE LESSONS I HAVE GIVEN YOU? ARE YOU WAITING FOR THE GOLDEN EGG TO COME ALONG? WELL, I MUST TELL YOU THAT THERE CAN BE NO GOLDEN EGG WITHOUT A GOOSE. MUST I GOOSE YOU?*"

We all had to admit that we hadn't been using the new tools like we could, so we made a new commitment to Sonny to incorporate our new tools more consistently in our daily lives. We have kept that commitment and now the situations we find ourselves in are getting easier and easier to deal with.

Not all of our old situations have changed, but many of them have.

We have been using many of the prior lessons to help us with this one. Some that have been really helpful are: 'I am Not This Body, I Am A Light Of God'; 'Writing A Difficult-To-Love Letter'; 'If You Can Think It, You Can Create It'; and 'I Get By With A Little Help From My Friends'. Oh, I almost forgot, 'The List' is probably the most helpful of all.

LESSON 28

CONNECTING WITH YOUR HIGHER SELF AND UNIVERSAL ENERGY

YOUR HIGHER SELF IS THE PART OF YOU THAT IS STILL PLUGGED INTO GOD. IT HAS A PERSONALITY, A NAME, AND A GREAT SENSE OF HUMOR. IT EXISTS IN LIGHT AS LIGHT; IT KNOWS YOUR MISSION IN THIS LIFE. IT KNOWS YOUR FEARS AND FAULTS AND LOVES YOU COMPLETELY, NONE-THE-LESS. IT IS THERE TO NURTURE, CARE, LOVE , AND GUIDE YOU ON YOUR PATH. CONNECTING WITH IT WILL FILL YOUR HEART AND MIND WITH A MOST BEAUTIFUL LIGHT. THIS WILL RAISE YOUR VIBRATION TO BURN OFF MUCH OF THE DEBRIS YOU HAVE ACCUMULATED IN YOUR LIFE, AND LEAVE YOU MUCH CLEARER ABOUT YOUR PURPOSE, YOUR GIFTS, AND THE NEXT STEPS YOU ARE TO TAKE ON YOUR PATH.

YOU MAY WANT TO SIT COMFORTABLY FOR THIS SHORT, BUT SWEET, EXERCISE I AM ABOUT TO GIVE YOU. CLOSE YOUR EYES, BREATHE IN DEEPLY, AND THEN EXHALE. LET GO OF EVERYTHING. GO BLANK. IMAGINE YOU ARE STARTING TO NOTICE A SMALL, REALLY BRIGHT LIGHT IN THE CORNER OF YOUR MIND'S IMAGE SCREEN. IT IS YOUR HIGHER SELF. SAY HELLO, THEN ALLOW YOUR HEART AND MIND TO OPEN AND SURRENDER TO THE LIGHT THAT IS YOUR HIGHER SELF.

THEN IMAGINE THAT LIGHT GROWING LARGER AND LARGER UNTIL IT TOTALLY SURROUNDS YOU. NOW YOU ARE INSIDE YOUR HIGHER SELF. FEEL THE LOVE, THE POWER. NOW INVITE IT IN. WITH EACH BREATH, FEEL THAT YOU ARE FILLING YOUR PHYSICAL BODY WITH THE GLORIOUS ESSENCE OF YOUR HIGHER SELF. FEEL IT FLOW THROUGH YOU, AND AS IT DOES, LET IT DISSOLVE AWAY ALL OF THE DARK, GRUNGY ENERGY YOU HAVE STUCK IN YOUR BEING, UNTIL YOU FEEL EVERY PART OF YOU IS GLOWING WITH RADIANCE. ENJOY THIS FEELING FOR SEVERAL MINUTES, ALLOWING YOURSELF TO BE AWARE OF ANY SPECIAL INSIGHTS, IMAGES, OR GUIDANCE. THEN SAY, "THANK YOU", STRETCH YOUR BODY, AND OPEN YOUR EYES. YOU HAVE CONNECTED!

IF YOUR HIGHER SELF APPEARS TO YOU AS MORE THAN LIGHT, FOR INSTANCE IN HUMAN FORM, IT WILL CHOOSE AN IMAGE, AND PERHAPS THE NAME OF ONE OF YOUR PAST LIVES IN WHICH YOU WERE CLOSELY CONNECTED WITH YOUR GOD SOURCE. THE CHOICE OF WHETHER TO APPEAR MALE OR FEMALE IS BASED ON WHICH GENDER WOULD INFLUENCE AND ATTRACT YOU TO IT. SOMETIMES IN CASES OF MUCH GROWTH, YOUR HIGHER SELF WILL SWITCH GENDER AND NAME TO SHOW YOU THE COMBINED ENERGIES IN ONE.

FOR THE UNIVERSAL ENERGY, CLOSE YOUR EYES AND IMAGINE THIS ENERGY RIGHT IN FRONT OF YOU. FEEL IT GROWING AND FLOWING INTO YOU AND BACK OUT AGAIN IN A CONSTANT FLOW. LIKE AN OCEAN FLOWING THROUGH YOU, EACH WAVE WASHES YOU CLEAN. PUT YOUR LOVE AND DESIRES OUT INTO THE UNIVERSE. FEEL

THE UNIVERSE, LIKE A FRESH WAVE, BRINGING IT BACK TO YOU. LET THIS ENERGY FLOW THROUGH YOU AND NOTICE THAT EACH TIME YOU GIVE LOVE, IT GIVES BACK.

SUMMARY

LESSON 28

Getting to know our Higher Selves has been an incredible experience. It is exciting to know that one day we will be merged with them.

We had amazing results doing this exercise. We all noticed a deep cleansing taking place within our bodies as they went about removing old debris.

I felt my Higher Self working on my throat area. I actually felt movement taking place there. It seemed as though it took a very long time before my throat felt free of this old energy. Eventually, I felt a light glow there. I sat and enjoyed this radiance of light inside my body for a long time. I was receiving instructions to speak up more and not to stuff my feelings and emotions, because they build up in that area. I knew and understood what my message was telling me.

Chris felt very expanded with no boundaries, as his Higher Self surrounded him. His Higher Self worked on his head and behind his eyes. He also felt a great deal of energy in his stomach area. As he sat with this radiance, he felt totally connected, very peaceful, and full of possibilities and potential. He had the feeling of, "Hey, I should do this more often."

Pat felt the light surrounding her with waves of profound peace and serenity. She said she had the thought that she had finally come home. Connecting with her Higher Self gave her a sense of security and safety. Whenever she feels jittery now she goes to her Higher Self and has an almost immediate sense of calmness.

Bess had no trouble surrounding herself with the light of her Higher Self. She described the feeling as being very comfortable and safe. Bringing her Higher Self into her was a little more difficult. She said that it took a number of times before she really felt the connection.

Since that first meditation, we have worked on getting a closer relationship established with our Higher Selves. We have learned a great deal about them and have come to understand their messages to us.

Adam is my Higher Self's name. I picture Adam with dark hair and a short beard. He wears a toga-like garment. He told me he appears to me as one of my past lifetimes in Atlantis. Adam is fun-loving and his most consistant message to me is to have more fun. Whenever I get too wrapped up in my work, or I start taking life too seriously, he gives me that message.

Charlemagne is Bess' Higher Self. Bess first saw Charlemagne as a beautiful, blonde goddess-like being, but more recently sees her as a brilliant, radiant light. There are times, too, when Bess just senses a strong connection taking place, or a message coming from her. Bess' most prevalent message from Charlemagne is to lighten up and look at the brighter side. Charlemagne sometimes does this by putting light, happy songs into her head. Bess loves music and this is a way of getting her attention.

Pat's Higher Self is Bartholomeow, but he says he prefers to be called Bart. Pat sees Bart as a huge, brilliant light in the shape of a potato. Bart's main message to Pat is to keep the lights burning bright. She understands this to mean to keep her light centers bright. (LESSON 32) Bart is concerned right now about Pat's health.

Yosef is Chris' Higher Self. Chris sees Yosef as a biblical prophet-like man with dark, curly hair and a long beard. He keeps reminding Chris that in order to become a known artist, he <u>must</u> paint. He tells Chris that just dreaming about painting does not cut it, but he must get busy and start doing it. He also reminds Chris that there are reasons for each circumstance in his life and he must look for the lesson rather than judge the circumstance.

Our Higher Selves have become very important in our lives, for it is their purpose to help us grow closer to our God

Selves. We strive to merge with them, as we continue to grow towards the Light.

Our experiences with Universal Energy were very similar. We all felt somewhat weightless as its waves washed through us. At the same time, we felt powerful and full of boundless love. We gave this energy our desires, but also our fears and doubts. The feelings after completing this exercise ranged from exhilaration to complete calmness.

LESSON 29

GOING FOR THE ESSENCE

SOMETIMES YOU TIGHTEN UP WHEN YOU HAVE DECISIONS TO MAKE. YOU HAVE CHOICES, BUT YOU KNOW NOT WHICH ONE TO MAKE. YOU WANT SOMETHING, BUT KNOW NOT HOW IT WOULD REALIZE ITSELF - CONFUSION REIGNS! SOMETIMES WHAT WOULD SOLVE YOUR CRISIS IS SOMETHING THAT YOUR FINITE MIND CANNOT UNDERSTAND OR CONCEIVE OF. THIS IS WHEN THIS LESSON WILL BE MOST MARVELLOUS.

SURE, YOU THINK YOU WANT THIS OR THAT, AND YOU THINK IT WILL GIVE YOU THIS OR THAT, AND SOMETIMES YOU EVEN GET WHAT YOU THOUGHT YOU WANTED, ONLY TO FIND IT DID NOT MAKE YOU HAPPY OR FILL THE NEED YOU THOUGHT IT WOULD. BUMMER, HUH? THIS IS PARTLY DUE TO THE FACT THAT YOU WENT AFTER SOMETHING WITHOUT FIRST KNOWING WHAT ESSENCES YOU WANTED IT TO SATISFY.

YOU HAVE LEARNED ABOUT THE HIGHER QUALITIES THAT YOU ARE SEEKING TO FULFILL IN WHAT YOU WANT TO MANIFEST, BUT THIS LESSON GOES ONE STEP FURTHER. FOR INSTANCE, IF YOU ARE LOOKING FOR MORE RELIABLE TRANSPORTATION, YOU MAY SAY, "OH, I NEED A NEW CAR", BUT THE ESSENCE IS REALLY RELIABILITY. *AND IF YOU MANIFEST THAT ESSENCE WITH THE QUALITIES IT WOULD GIVE YOU, SUCH AS FREEDOM AND JOY, THEN YOU MAY FIND YOUR OLD CAR RUNNING FINE AND YOU COULD HAVE SPENT A LOT OF MONEY ON ANOTHER CAR THAT WAS JUST AS UNRELIABLE. IF YOU WANT A NEW HOME, WHAT WOULD THE ROOMS BE USED BE FOR? WHAT KIND OF SPACE DO YOU NEED? WHAT IS THE COST PER MONTH? WHAT OTHER FEATURES DO YOU WANT? WHAT OTHER ESSENCES? AND WHAT ABOUT A GREAT JOB? YOU KNOW NOT THE SPECIFICS, BUT YOU DO KNOW THAT YOU WANT TO USE YOUR GIFTS, YOU WANT A CERTAIN SALARY, FRIENDLY PEOPLE, AND A PLEASANT ATMOSPHERE. THESE ESSENCES, ALONG WITH THE HIGHER QUALITIES YOU WANT WILL GET YOU SOMETHING EVEN BETTER THAN YOU COULD IMAGINE.*

THE FIRST THING YOU NEED TO DO IS TO KNOW BOTH THE ESSENCES AND THE HIGHER QUALITIES THAT YOU WANT SOMETHING TO GIVE YOU, BECAUSE IF YOU DO NOT, THEN YOU WILL JUST BE DOING THINGS THE SAME OLD WAY. WHAT I HAVE FOR YOU IS SOMETHING TOTALLY NEW. IT IS A TOTALLY NEW WAY TO BRING SOMETHING OR SOMEONE INTO YOUR LIFE. I CALL IT 'ANGELTIZING'. TO START, CALL IN YOUR HIGHER SELF, AND FROM THAT PLACE OF TOTAL CONNECTION, VISUALIZE WHAT YOU WANT. IF YOU KNOW NOT THE SPECIFIC FORM IT WILL TAKE, THEN ALLOW A SYMBOL TO SUBSTITUTE. THEN ADD THE ESSENCES OF IT AND THE HIGHER QUALITIES YOU WANT IT TO HELP YOU EXPRESS. BE SURE TO SEE YOURSELF IN THE PICTURE, ALONG WITH THE THING OR PERSON, ENJOYING THE ESSENCES AND HIGHER QUALITIES, UNTIL YOU CAN ALMOST SENSE WHAT YOU WANT IN FRONT OF YOU.

NOW COMES THE FUN PART - ANGELTIZING. FROM YOUR LEFT AND RIGHT, SEND OUT A LINE OF ANGELS WITH HANDS LINKED TOGETHER IN A CHAIN THAT GOES OUT

FROM YOU AND ENCIRCLES WHAT YOU ARE VISUALIZING. THE ANGELS WILL SHINE A BRIGHT LIGHT ON IT, ADDING THEIR OWN ESSENCES AND HIGHER QUALITIES. SLOWLY THEY BEGIN TO DRAW IT NEARER TO YOU.

DECIDE WHERE YOU WANT THE IMAGE YOU HAVE ANGELTIZED TO COME IN. YOU MAY CHOOSE YOUR HEART OR YOUR HANDS OR ALL AROUND YOU. IF THE ANGELS CAN ONLY BRING IT SO FAR, THEN MAYBE YOU ARE NOT QUITE READY TO RECEIVE IT, OR YOU HAVE CERTAIN OTHER STEPS TO TAKE FIRST. AT THIS POINT, ASK YOUR HIGHER SELF WHAT ELSE YOU NEED TO KNOW OR DO. YOU MAY GET A PICTURE, OR A KNOWINGNESS RIGHT AWAY OR IN A FEW DAYS. SPEND THE NEXT FEW DAYS LOOKING FOR SIGNS AND ACTING AS THOUGH IT HAS ALREADY BEEN GRANTED. SOMETIMES THEY CAN BRING IT RIGHT INTO YOU. WHAT DOES IT FEEL LIKE? THIS MEANS THAT YOU ARE READY TO RECEIVE IT AND IT WILL COME SOON.

ONE THING I WANT TO ADD IS BE SURE YOU WANT WHAT YOU ARE ANGELTIZING, AND BE WILLING TO DO WHAT MAY BE NECESSARY TO GET IT. START WITH SMALL THINGS YOU KNOW YOU CAN CREATE EASILY. YOU MUST BE ABLE TO HONESTLY BELIEVE *THAT YOU CAN CREATE IT. YOU MAY WANT A MILLION DOLLARS, BUT IS THAT NOT A WEE BIT MUCH WHEN YOU CANNOT IMAGINE PAYING THE RENT ON TIME?*

BE SURE TO LOVE WHAT YOU ARE ANGELTIZING AND GET EXCITED ABOUT IT. YOU MAY THINK YOU SHOULD ANGELTIZE MONEY TO PAY THE BILLS. WELL, 'SHOULDS' ARE NOT EXCITING AND DO NOT COME FROM YOUR HIGHER SELF. ALSO, WHEN STARTING OUT, PICK THINGS YOU DO NOT NEED, BUT RATHER ARE DETACHED ABOUT. THAT WAY, IT IS NO BIG DEAL IF YOU RECEIVE IT OR NOT. WHEN ANGELTIZING PEOPLE, SUCH AS CLIENTS OR CUSTOMERS, CONNECT WITH THEIR HEART INSTEAD OF FOCUSING ON WHAT THEY WILL GIVE YOU. SEND OUT WHAT YOU WILL BE DOING FOR THEIR HIGHEST GOOD. PRACTICE AND HAVE FUN WITH THIS, AND KNOW YOUR ANGELS WANT YOU TO HAVE EVERYTHING YOU WANT, AND THAT THEY WILL HELP YOU ALL THEY CAN.

SUMMARY

LESSON 29

We have had some wonderful successes with Angeltizing, but we have also had some disappointments, which caused us to ask Sonny for more clarity.

Pat was having difficulty with this lesson because she had trouble visualizing. Sonny was able to help her by giving her this advice, "*THIS IS REALLY NO PROBLEM. YOU HAVE MANY OTHER SENSES THAT CAN SUBSTITUTE FOR VISUALIZATION. TRY FEELING, SENSING, IMAGINING, PRETENDING, KNOWING, BELIEVING, AND OF COURSE, SMELLING AND TASTING. TRY TO ANGELTIZE THINGS WHERE YOU WOULD BE ABLE TO USE SEVERAL SENSES, AND REMEMBER THAT THE HIGHER QUALITIES AND ESSENCES ARE MOSTLY FEELINGS ANYWAY*".

Another problem we encountered was the amount of time it took for our Angeltizing to work. Sometimes it would work very quickly, and at other times it seemed to take forever, or it just didn't happen at all. Sonny gave us insights into timing. "*WHEN YOU ANGELTIZE SOMETHING, THE AMOUNT OF TIME DEPENDS ON A NUMBER OF THINGS: HOW WILLING ARE YOU? DO YOU BELIEVE YOU DESERVE IT YET? DO YOU BELIEVE IT IS POSSIBLE? HAVE YOU BEEN LISTENING TO GUIDANCE AS TO WHAT STEPS TO TAKE, OR WHAT YOU NEED TO LEARN, OR CHANGE FIRST? ARE YOU REALLY SURE YOU KNOW WHAT YOU WANT? HAVE YOU REALLY THOUGHT ABOUT IT AND FELT THE ESSENCES AND HIGHER QUALITIES? ARE YOU SURE YOU WANT IT? WOULD IT BE GOOD FOR YOUR GROWTH? ARE YOU TRULY OPEN TO RECEIVE? YOU CANNOT PICK-UP A HANDFUL OF GOLDEN COINS IF YOUR FISTS ARE CLENCHED IN FEAR OF - WHAT IF IT DOES NOT WORK, INSTEAD OF THE OPEN ARMS AND HANDS OF ONE WHO SAYS, 'I AM READY TO RECEIVE AND I KNOW THAT IT IS A COMIN'.*"

At a later date, Sonny expanded on this more. "*WHEN YOU ASK FOR SOMETHING AND IT IS FOR YOUR HIGHEST GOOD, IT WILL*

FLOW AND YOU WILL RECEIVE SIGNS IMMEDIATELY. YOU CAN ALWAYS GO AHEAD AND CREATE IT ANYWAY, BUT IT MAY TAKE LONGER AND NOT GIVE YOU WHAT YOU WANT. SO WHEN YOU ASK, LET GO. AND WHEN YOU GET A SIGN, TAKE WHATEVER ACTION IS CALLED FOR."

What we have discovered on our own is that sometimes our enthusiasm brought the Angels in too quickly. We have learned to let them come to us more slowly and to pay close attention to any hesitation that might occur as they approached. At that point, we then ask our Higher Selves if there is more we should know in regards to what we are trying to Angeltize. So when Angeltizing, be sure to bring the Angels in slowly so you are aware of any hesitation or stopping along the way.

It is important that you do the processing before Angeltizing. Ask yourself those questions Sonny mentioned. Know what you want and why you want it. Doing this processing has helped us create many more successes and has also helped us to realize that some of the things we wanted weren't for our highest good, or the highest good of all concerned.

LESSON 30

LEARN TO DISCERN

DISCERNMENT, MY FRIENDS, IS WHAT YOU NEED TO DEVELOP IN ORDER TO MAKE ACCURATE, CONSCIOUS CHOICES IN YOUR LIFE. 'DOES IT RESONATE?' IS THE QUESTION TO ASK. THIS IS TO HELP YOU DETERMINE WHAT IS TRUE GUIDANCE. IT IS NOT ONLY IMPOSSIBLE TO KEEP ALL BUT TRUE GUIDANCE FROM YOU, BUT ALSO AN INVASION OF YOUR FREE WILL TO DO SO.

THE UNIVERSAL REFEREE IS NOT GOING TO SHOUT "FOUL" EACH TIME AN UNAUTHORIZED PLAYER ENTERS THE FIELD. YOU WILL ALWAYS HAVE CHOICES. YOUR GROWTH INVOLVES DISCERNING WHICH CHOICES ARE FOR YOU AND WHICH ARE NOT.

YOUR HIGHER SELF KNOWS YOUR HIGHEST PURPOSE AND THE STEPS YOU NEED TO TAKE TO GET THERE, BUT IN

TRYING TO CONVEY THEM TO YOU, USELESS JUNK CLOGS UP YOUR CHANNELS.

I HAVE A FUN LITTLE GAME FOR YOU TO PLAY. SINCE IT IS MOST ESSENTIAL FOR YOUR GROWTH TO LEARN TO FIND YOUR OWN ANSWERS, I HAVE DESIGNED THIS GAME SPECIFICALLY TO SHOW YOU WHAT YOU ALREADY KNOW. YOU MAY HAVE GLIMPSED YOUR HIGHER PURPOSE AND MAY ALREADY BE DOING IT, BUT MAY NOT HAVE ACCEPTED IT AS YOUR PATH. I TELL YOU THAT YOUR PATH OF MOST LIGHT, AND THE STEPS YOU NEED TO TAKE, ARE NOT REALLY NEW AND MAY NOT SURPRISE YOU BECAUSE YOU ALREADY KNOW IT AND RESONATE TO IT. WITH IT, YOU CAN GET EXCITED AND FEEL GOOD ABOUT COMMITTING YOURSELF TO IT.

SO THE GAME THEN, IS TO SIT QUIETLY AND CONNECT TO YOUR HIGHER SELF. THEN, WITH YOUR MIND AND PERSONALITY OUT OF THE WAY, LET YOUR HIGHER SELF SPEAK TO YOU OR SHOW YOU WHAT IT IS THAT YOU TRULY RESONATE TO AND ALSO SHOW YOU THE NEXT STEPS THAT YOU ARE TO TAKE. WRITE IT DOWN AND SEE IF IT RESONATES. THEN START DOING THESE STEPS SO THAT YOU CAN START DOING WHAT YOU ARE HERE TO DO.

SUMMARY

LESSON 30

Discernment is not as easy as it sounds. We have come to understand that it is more of a gut-level reaction to something than anything else. It is not always something that is logical. No matter what our rational minds tell us, discernment comes from a deeper part of ourselves.

Prior to receiving this lesson, Sonny helped Chris and I to understand why we had believed we were being guided to Brazil. The fact that it did not happen was what confused us. We thought we were getting signs to go, even though, deep inside, it was not something that felt right. Sonny is exaggerating here with this explanation, but it did help us to understand how we can misinterpret what we think of as signs. "*YOU HAVE BEEN THINKING ABOUT BRAZIL FOR THREE MONTHS. YOU CAN BAKE A BRAZILIAN DESSERT, YOU KNOW A BRAZILIAN RESTAURANT, SO YOU ARE BEING GUIDED TO START A BRAZILIAN DESSERT SHOP, AND OF COURSE, IT WILL HAVE TO BE IN MIAMI BECAUSE YOU STAYED THERE BEFORE AND MANY BRAZILIANS PASS THROUGH MIAMI. YOU VOLUNTEER WHERE YOU SEE AN ELDERLY WOMAN DOING AEROBICS, LATER YOU SEE A COMMERCIAL FOR JANE FONDA WORKOUT TAPES. YOU ARE BEING GUIDED TO TEACH AN AEROBICS CLASS. DOES THIS RESONATE?*" We were beginning to understand. Sonny had us do this lesson right away. He had us write down what we had received and then come back to the Angel Talk Board so that he could make comments and ask questions to help us get ready for the 'right stuff', as he put it. He said, "*MY POINTERS WILL SERVE AS USEFUL TOOLS FOR OTHERS.*"

We all received information, although we weren't sure if all we received was correct. Here is what each of us received and what Sonny had to say about our information.

Pat was first and this is what she received: "Find a job where you can help others have a better way of life. In this way, you will help yourself to a better way of life. In your spare time, make heavenly jewelry for heavenly people. There is a definite market for it." Sonny's comments: "*WHAT DO YOU FEEL? THE FIRST PART IS DEFINITELY YOUR CALLING. HOW WONDERFUL! THE SECOND PART IS YOU WAKING UP TO YOUR GIFTS, AND MAY I SUGGEST THAT YOU FIND A GROUP THAT REGULARLY DOES TOUCH HEALING TO HELP YOU MORE FULLY EXPRESS YOUR INNATE DESIRE TO MAKE THE "OWEE" GO AWAY.*" Pat was very pleased with Sonny's comments and began looking into finding a group to learn more about healing.

Bess was next and received this information: "Poems, music, fun, light, spiritual path, greatness, what you are doing now." (At the time of this lesson, Bess was having trouble wanting or desiring to find a job. She had just discovered her gift of writing poetry and was having too much fun doing that.) Sonny's comments: "*THE POEMS THAT INSPIRE AND ILLUSTRATE SPIRITUAL QUALITIES OR LESSONS - THIS IS YOUR HIGHEST PATH. AS YOU BEGIN TO CHANNEL HIGHER VIBRATIONS, OTHER ABILITIES WILL SURFACE. FIND YOUR OWN UNIQUE STYLE. LEARN TO DISCERN BETWEEN REAL GUIDANCE, AND EGO MASQUERADING AS AN ANGEL TO JUSTIFY NON ACTION. WHILE WORKING ON YOUR HIGHER GIFTS, YOU STILL NEED TO PUT BREAD ON THE TABLE. YOU MUST TAKE CARE OF YOUR BASICS FIRST. MAKE A DECISION TO WORK. IT REALLY IS A PART OF YOUR PATH.*" Bess really did feel her hesitation came from the Angels, but now she is able to distinguish between what is real guidance and what are her ego's messages.

I was next and this is what I received: "Write, write, write. After "An Angel's Guide to Heaven on Earth", you will have more that you will want to write. Take a word processing class, or buy a book on the subject, so that you can learn to use your new machine." Sonny's comments: "*OH, SUSAN, ARE YOU GREAT OR WHAT? WAS IT NOT THAT WHICH HAS RESONATED WITH YOU FOR YEARS? BUT WHAT SHALL YOU WRITE?*" (I said that I would like to write something spiritual.) "*AND DO YOU HAVE THIS MATERIAL IN MIND?*" (No, not really.) "*GEE, WHERE WOULD YOU IMAGINE IT WOULD COME FROM? WHAT HAVE YOU SECRETLY WANTED TO DO AND ALREADY DO, BUT DENY THAT YOU DO IT?*" (I had no idea.) "*BEAUTIFULLY CHANNELED, INSPIRATIONAL WRITING. WHAT IF I TOLD YOU THAT IF YOU REALLY COMMITTED TO IT, YOU WOULD BE*

PULLING IN SOME REALLY GREAT STUFF FROM VERY HIGH TEACHERS OF THE LIGHT?" (That sounded fantastic to me!) *"SO BE IT! I WILL EXPECT NOTHING LESS FROM YOU. AND I KNOW THAT YOU ARE CONCERNED ABOUT YOUR SURVIVAL, TOO, BUT THE REMAINDER OF THE YEAR WILL BE ENOUGH TO GET YOU GOING; THEN FUN PART-TIME EMPLOYMENT WILL SERVE TO ENHANCE YOUR LIFE. THE WORD PROCESSING CLASS SEEMS UNNECESSARY - A PRODUCT OF YOUR DOUBTS ABOUT YOUR ABILITIES. YOU MAY SPEAK LATER AS A CONSCIOUS CHANNEL, AND DO NOT FORGET THE BRAZILIAN DESSERT SHOP!"* (Ha ha!)

Now it was Chris' turn. This is what he received: "My highest purpose is to use my gifts to touch people's hearts and bring them to new realizations. Steps are to paint, do illustrations, cards, stories, etc." Sonny's comments: *"TOUCH PEOPLE'S HEARTS AND BRING THEM TO NEW REALIZATIONS WITH YOUR GIFTS? GIVE THE MAN A KEWPIE DOLL! GEE, YOU MUST HAVE HAD SOME HELP. DO YOU MIND IF I JOKE WITH YOU? REALIZE THAT YOUR WORK IS BECOMING MORE POWERFUL. DO NOT UNDER SELL YOUR TALENT. ALSO, ANYTHING GIVEN FROM THE HEART WILL ACT AS A PROSPERITY MAGNET FOR YOU."*

We were amazed that we were able to find out this information on our own, with the help of our Higher Selves, that is. It was a little surprising to find that much of what we considered hobbies were actually a part of our higher purpose. The trick with discernment is to listen, but then to go deeper for a gut reaction. We don't always get it right; sometimes our own desires get in the way. Also, another point to consider, is that we are now playing a new game with new rules. Don't forget to consider if it is for the highest good of all concerned. Discernment isn't always easy, but we are working at it.

LESSON 31

PLAYING WITH LIGHT

YOU CAN CHANGE YOUR SOCKS; YOU CAN CHANGE CHANNELS ON THE TELEVISION; YOU CAN CHANGE DIAPERS; YOU CAN CHANGE YOUR MIND - ALL WITHIN A MATTER OF SECONDS OR MINUTES. NOW YOU CAN JUST AS EASILY CHANGE YOUR PERSONAL ENERGY, THE ENERGY IN THE ROOM, OR THE ENERGY OF THE ENTIRE PLANET. LIGHT IS ENERGY AND DIFFERENT COLORS OF LIGHT AFFECT YOU IN DIFFERENT WAYS. SOME COLORS OF LIGHT WILL RELAX YOU, SOME WILL MAKE YOU FEEL MORE LOVE, SOME WILL MAKE YOU FEEL MORE PEACEFUL, SOME WILL HELP WITH MENTAL WORK, AND SOME WITH SPIRITUAL GROWTH. WHEN YOU CHANGE THE COLOR OF LIGHT THAT SURROUNDS YOU, YOU CAN GAIN MORE CONTROL OVER WHAT AND HOW YOU FEEL. THERE ARE SOME FUN EXERCISES YOU CAN DO TO EXPERIENCE THE DIFFERENT EF-

FECTS COLORED LIGHT ENERGY HAS ON YOUR FEELINGS AND MOODS.

SIT COMFORTABLY WITH YOUR EYES CLOSED. ABOVE YOU IS A WONDERFUL INVENTION - A SHOWER HEAD THAT SPRAYS A FINE MIST OF COLORED LIGHT. NOW IMAGINE THIS SHOWER HEAD TURNING ON AND SPRAYING A MOST BEAUTIFUL PASTEL PINK LIGHT ALL OVER YOU. BREATHE DEEPLY AND FEEL THE PINK LIGHT FILL YOU AND PENETRATE EVERY CELL. FEEL IT IN A MARVELLOUS MISTY BUBBLE SEVERAL FEET ALL AROUND YOU. HOW DOES IT FEEL? IS IT DIFFERENT THAN IT WAS A FEW MOMENTS BEFORE? DO YOU LIKE THE PINK LIGHT? NOW SWITCH THE SHOWER HEAD TO A LOVELY PASTEL BLUE LIGHT AND EXPERIENCE IT IN THE SAME WAY AS THE PINK. HOW DOES THE BLUE LIGHT FEEL? DO YOU LIKE IT? TRY A COUPLE MORE COLORS, (LIGHT PASTELS ARE BEST). NOTICE HOW AND WHAT EACH COLOR MAKES YOU FEEL. PICK YOUR FAVORITE COLOR AND STAND UP AND WALK AROUND. NOTICE THE COLORED LIGHT MIST STAYS WITH YOU, NO MATTER HOW FAST YOU MOVE. IS IT NOT GREAT?

NOW PICK SOMEONE AT A DISTANCE FROM YOU, SOMEONE YOU FEEL MIGHT BENEFIT FROM A CHANGE OF LIGHT. IT COULD BE SOMEONE YOU KNOW, OR A STRANGER, SUCH AS SOMEONE THAT YOU HAVE HEARD ABOUT WHO IS HAVING PROBLEMS, OR EVEN A WORLD LEADER. NOW IMAGINE THEM WITH A SHOWER HEAD ABOVE THEM, SPRAYING THEM WITH COLORED LIGHT. TRY A COLOR THAT FEELS GOOD TO YOU AT FIRST, THEN YOU MAY BE GUIDED TO CHANGE THE COLOR. SATURATE THEM ALL OVER! (THIS IS A WONDERFUL WAY TO HAVE FUN WHILE HELPING FOLKS.)

NOW IMAGINE A BIG SHOWER HEAD ABOVE THE ROOM YOU ARE IN. FILL THE ROOM WITH A COLOR OF LIGHT THAT YOU LIKE. FEEL HOW DIFFERENT THE ROOM IS. YOU CAN DO THIS AT YOUR OFFICE OR WORKPLACE BEFORE YOU GET THERE. THEN WALK IN AND EXPERIENCE A TOTALLY NEW FEELING. FIND OUT WHICH COLOR OF LIGHT HELPS YOU SLEEP BEST AND FILL YOUR BEDROOM WITH IT.

FINALLY, IMAGINE A HUGE SHOWER HEAD OUT IN SPACE, AIMED AT THE EARTH. HAVE IT SPRAY WHATEVER COLOR OF LIGHT MIST THAT YOUR GUIDANCE SUGGESTS. SOME PLACES ON THE PLANET MAY NEED MORE THAN ONE COLOR. SOAK IT GOOD. HAVE FUN PLAYING WITH THE LIGHT.

SUMMARY

LESSON 31

We use this lesson almost daily for a number of reasons. It is very effective in helping us change our own moods as well as changing the negative moods of others, and it works quickly and has lasting affects.

I have been using this exercise for the conflicts that are happening in our world. I am continually spraying those areas of the world where conflicts are taking place. I also spray pastel pink on the leaders of each country involved. One leader, that I will not mention by name, has been fighting me on this. He keeps disappearing on me and will not permit me to spray him. I could not understand this and so I decided to ask Sonny about it. Here is what he said: "*IF HE ALLOWED ENERGIES OF PEACE TO CHANGE HIS ATTITUDE, THERE IS GREAT DANGER, HE FEARS, THAT HE WILL BELIEVE HIMSELF WRONG FOR MAKING WAR IN THE FIRST PLACE, AND WE ALL KNOW HE HATES TO BE MADE WRONG. TRY STARTING TO IGNITE A SPARK OF LOVE RIGHT IN THE CENTER OF HIM AND LET IT GROW, INSTEAD OF CHASING HIM AROUND WITH HUMBLING PINK LIGHT.*" I have done this and have noticed a slight change.

Chris uses this technique at work and has noticed very significant changes in his environment. The people are less stressed and more positive. When he sprays his own area, he feels more in control of his surroundings and less subject to the negativity that may be going on around him.

We have had a lot of success with this lesson. We have tested it out with many different situations and people. It always has a positive effect. You will find that different colors affect different people in different ways. One particular color will not mean the same thing to everyone. Asking for guidance as to what color is best to use really helps. I might try one that I like and right in the middle of spraying, it will change to a different color. I know that this is guidance and I do not question it. This lesson is not only helpful, but lots of fun as well.

LESSON 32

THE SEVEN MAJOR LIGHT CENTERS

WE WILL NOW FOCUS ON THE SEVEN MAJOR LIGHT CENTERS IN YOUR LIGHT BODY. IMAGINE A GOLDEN ELECTRICAL CORD HANGING DOWN FROM THE CEILING ABOVE YOU. HIGH ABOVE THAT IS A HUGE ENERGY SOURCE LIKE A POWER STATION. THIS IS GOD. IMAGINE A PLUG-IN SOMEWHERE AND NOTICE THAT THIS IS WHERE YOUR GOLDEN ELECTRICAL CORD BEGINS. FOLLOW THIS CORD DOWN TO WHERE IT IS JUST ABOVE YOUR HEAD. NOTICE THAT HERE IS A LIGHT SOCKET. THIS IS YOUR FIRST LIGHT CENTER IN YOUR LIGHT BODY. NOW CALL UPON YOUR GUARDIAN ANGEL TO ASSIST YOU IN CONNECTING WITH AND UNDERSTANDING THE FUNCTION OF YOUR LIGHT CENTER. YOUR ANGEL TAKES A FLASHLIGHT FROM THE POCKET OF HIS/HER GOWN AND SHINES IT ON THIS LIGHT SOCKET ABOVE YOUR HEAD. YOU SUDDENLY BE-

COME AWARE THAT THE FUNCTION OF YOUR FIRST LIGHT CENTER IS TO RECEIVE SPIRITUAL GUIDANCE. YOUR ANGEL BEGINS TO REMOVE SOME OF THE COBWEBS AND DEAD BUGS AND DIRT FROM YOUR FIRST LIGHT SOCKET. THESE ARE YOUR OLD BLOCKAGES, OLD FEARS, AND BELIEFS. YOUR ANGEL PLACES ALL OF THIS DEBRIS IN THE GOLDEN BOWL OF TRANSMUTATION AT HIS/HER FEET. IT IMMEDIATELY BURSTS INTO A BRILLIANT VIOLET FLAME. WHEN THE FLAME DIES DOWN, YOUR ANGEL REACHES INTO THE BOWL AND FINDS A LOVELY VIOLET LIGHT BULB. THEN YOUR ANGEL INSERTS THIS BULB INTO THE LIGHT SOCKET ABOVE YOUR HEAD, AND AFTER GIVING IT A FEW TURNS, IT SHINES WITH A MOST BEAUTIFUL VIOLET LIGHT. FEEL THIS VIOLET LIGHT PENETRATE THROUGH THE CROWN OF YOUR HEAD. YOU ARE READY TO RECEIVE, IN ABUNDANCE, HIGHER KNOWING, HIGHER UNDERSTANDING, AND SPIRITUAL GUIDANCE. SIT WITH THIS FEELING FOR AS LONG AS YOU LIKE. GUIDANCE MAY COME FOR YOU NOW OR UNFOLD FOR YOU LATER.

NOW IMAGINE THIS CORD EXTENDING DOWN FROM YOUR FIRST LIGHT CENTER, THROUGH YOUR CROWN AND DOWN THROUGH THE CENTER OF YOU, ALL THE WAY TO YOUR TAIL BONE. YOUR ANGEL THEN TAKES THE FLASHLIGHT AND THIS TIME SHINES IT DIRECTLY AT YOUR FOREHEAD. HERE IS YOUR SECOND LIGHT CENTER. YOU BECOME AWARE THAT THE FUNCTION OF THIS LIGHT CENTER IS TO HELP YOU EXPERIENCE HIGHER VISION. YOUR ANGEL THEN BEGINS TO REMOVE ALL OF THE OLD DEBRIS FROM AROUND THIS SECOND LIGHT SOCKET AND PLACES IT INTO THE GOLDEN BOWL OF TRANSMUTATION. IT IMMEDIATELY BURSTS INTO A BRILLIANT WHITE FLAME WITH FLASHES OF GOLD. WHEN THE FLAME HAS DIED, YOUR ANGEL REACHES INTO THE BOWL AND FINDS A LOVELY WHITE BULB WITH GOLD FLECKS. AS YOUR ANGEL INSERTS THIS BULB INTO YOUR FOREHEAD, IT SHINES WITH A MOST BEAUTIFUL WHITE AND GOLD LIGHT. FEEL THIS LIGHT PENETRATE YOUR MIND AND EYES. YOU ARE NOW READY TO RECEIVE HIGHER VISION IN ABUNDANCE. FEEL THIS

FEELING FOR AS LONG AS YOU LIKE. GUIDANCE MAY COME NOW OR UNFOLD FOR YOU LATER.

YOUR ANGEL NOW TAKES THE FLASHLIGHT AND PLACES IT AT YOUR THROAT. HERE IS ANOTHER LIGHT SOCKET, FOR THIS IS YOUR THIRD LIGHT CENTER. YOU BECOME AWARE THAT THE FUNCTION OF THIS CENTER IS TO HELP YOU EXPERIENCE HIGHER COMMUNICATION AND TO REACH OUT. YOUR ANGEL THEN STARTS REMOVING THE DEBRIS FROM AROUND YOUR THROAT, MOUTH, AND EARS. THESE AREAS ARE VERY IMPORTANT IN OPENING UP TO HIGHER COMMUNICATION. THEN YOUR ANGEL BEGINS REMOVING DEBRIS FROM AROUND YOUR SHOULDERS, ELBOWS, ARMS, WRISTS, HANDS, AND YOUR FINGERS. THIS IS TO PREPARE YOU FOR REACHING OUT AND TOUCHING AND HEALING. THE ANGEL DUMPS IT ALL INTO THE GOLDEN BOWL OF TRANSMUTATION. THE DEBRIS BURSTS INTO A BRILLIANT PASTEL BLUE FLAME. WHEN THE FLAME DIES DOWN, YOUR ANGEL REACHES INTO THE BOWL AND FINDS A LOVELY PASTEL BLUE LIGHT BULB. YOUR ANGEL INSERTS THIS BULB INTO YOUR THROAT AND IT SHINES WITH THE MOST BRILLIANT PASTEL BLUE LIGHT. FEEL THIS LIGHT PENETRATE YOUR THROAT, MOUTH, AND EARS. THEN FEEL IT TRAVEL THROUGH YOUR JAWS, NECK, AND OUTWARD THROUGH YOUR SHOULDERS, ELBOWS, ARMS, WRISTS, HANDS, AND YOUR FINGERS. IMAGINE THIS LIGHT SHINING OUT THROUGH THE PALMS OF YOUR HANDS AND OUT THROUGH YOUR FINGER TIPS. YOU ARE READY TO RECEIVE HIGHER COMMUNICATION AND YOU ARE READY TO REACH OUT TO TOUCH, HOLD, AND HEAL. SIT WITH THIS FEELING FOR AS LONG AS YOU LIKE. GUIDANCE MAY COME NOW OR UNFOLD FOR YOU LATER.

WITH GREAT JOY, YOUR ANGEL NOW SHINES THE FLASHLIGHT IN THE CENTER OF YOUR HEART. HERE IS ANOTHER LIGHT CENTER. YOU BECOME AWARE THAT THE FUNCTION OF THIS LIGHT CENTER IS TO HELP YOU EXPERIENCE HIGHER LOVE AND A LOVING WILL. YOUR ANGEL BEGINS TO REMOVE ALL OF THE OLD DEBRIS FROM AROUND YOUR HEART AND DEPOSITS IT IN THE GOLDEN BOWL OF TRANSMUTATION, WHERE IT BURSTS INTO THE

MOST BRILLIANT PINK FLAME. WHEN THE FLAME HAS DIED, YOUR ANGEL REACHES INTO THE BOWL AND REMOVES A LOVELY PINK LIGHT BULB. THEN YOUR ANGEL INSERTS IT INTO THE LIGHT SOCKET IN YOUR HEART AND IT SHINES WITH A MOST BEAUTIFUL PINK LIGHT. FEEL THE LIGHT PENETRATE AS IT RADIATES OUT FROM YOUR HEART. YOU ARE NOW READY TO RECEIVE AND GIVE HIGHER LOVE AND TO USE YOUR LOVING WILL. THIS IS DIFFERENT FROM YOUR FORCEFUL WILL, YOUR WILL POWER, WHICH IS CENTERED IN YOUR SOLAR PLEXUS. YOU HAVE EVOLVED TO A LEVEL WHERE YOU ARE NOW USING THE GENTLE POWER OF YOUR LOVING WILL TO BRING ABOUT THE CHANGES YOU WANT TO MAKE IN AN EASIER, MORE LOVING WAY THAN EVER BEFORE. SIT WITH THIS FEELING FOR AS LONG AS YOU LIKE. GUIDANCE MAY COME NOW OR UNFOLD FOR YOU LATER.

YOUR ANGEL NOW TAKES THE FLASHLIGHT AND SHINES IT ON YOUR SOLAR PLEXUS. THIS IS YOUR FIFTH LIGHT CENTER. YOU BECOME AWARE THAT THE FUNCTION OF THIS CENTER IS TO HELP YOU EXPERIENCE HIGHER CREATIVITY AND PHYSICAL ENERGY. YOUR ANGEL THEN STARTS TO REMOVE THE DEBRIS FROM AROUND THIS CENTER AND DROPS IT INTO THE GOLDEN BOWL OF TRANSMUTATION. IT BURSTS INTO A MOST BRILLIANT GOLDEN FLAME. WHEN THE FLAME DIES DOWN, YOUR ANGEL FINDS A LOVELY GOLDEN-YELLOW LIGHT BULB. YOUR ANGEL TAKES THIS BULB AND INSERTS IT INTO THE LIGHT SOCKET. IT SHINES WITH A MOST BEAUTIFUL GOLDEN-YELLOW LIGHT. FEEL THIS GOLDEN-YELLOW LIGHT PENETRATE AND RADIATE OUT FROM YOUR SOLAR PLEXUS. YOU ARE NOW READY TO RECEIVE HIGHER CREATIVITY AND PHYSICAL ENERGY. SIT WITH THIS FEELING AS LONG AS YOU LIKE. GUIDANCE MAY COME NOW OR UNFOLD FOR YOU LATER.

YOUR ANGEL NOW TAKES THE FLASHLIGHT AND POINTS IT AT YOUR LOWER ABDOMEN. HERE IS ANOTHER LIGHT SOCKET, FOR THIS IS YOUR SIXTH LIGHT CENTER. YOU MAY BECOME AWARE THAT THE FUNCTION OF THIS CENTER IS TO HELP YOU EXPERIENCE HIGHER SENSITIVITY

AND EMOTIONAL BALANCE. YOUR ANGEL JOYFULLY REMOVES ALL OF THE OLD DEBRIS AND DROPS IT INTO THE GOLDEN BOWL OF TRANSMUTATION, WHERE IT BURSTS INTO A MOST BRILLIANT ORANGE FLAME. WHEN THE FLAME HAS DIED, YOUR ANGEL REACHES INTO THE BOWL AND REMOVES A MOST MARVELLOUS ORANGE LIGHT BULB. THEN YOUR ANGEL INSERTS THIS INTO YOUR LIGHT SOCKET JUST BELOW YOUR BELLY BUTTON AND IT GLOWS WITH A MOST BEAUTIFUL ORANGE LIGHT. YOU ARE NOW READY TO RECEIVE HIGHER SENSITIVITY AND EMOTIONAL BALANCE. SIT WITH THIS FEELING FOR AS LONG AS YOU LIKE. GUIDANCE MAY COME NOW OR UNFOLD FOR YOU LATER.

YOUR ANGEL TAKES THE FLASHLIGHT ONE MORE TIME AND SHINES IT AT YOUR GROIN AREA. HERE AT THE END OF THE GOLDEN ELECTRIC CORD IS THE LAST LIGHT SOCKET, AND YOUR SEVENTH LIGHT CENTER. YOU BECOME AWARE THAT THE FUNCTION OF THIS CENTER IS TO HELP YOU EXPERIENCE HIGHER TRANSFORMATION OF ENERGIES, QUICKER AND EASIER RELEASE OF THE OLD, AND HIGHER MANIFESTATION OF YOUR NEEDS AND DESIRES. YOUR ANGEL QUICKLY REMOVES ALL OF THE OLD DEBRIS FROM THIS AREA AND DEPOSITS IT INTO THE GOLDEN BOWL OF TRANSMUTATION, WHERE IT INSTANTLY BURST INTO A HOT, RED FLAME. WHEN THE FLAME HAS DIED, YOUR ANGEL REACHES INTO THE BOWL AND FINDS A MOST WONDERFUL RED LIGHT BULB. THEN YOUR ANGEL INSERTS IT INTO THE LIGHT SOCKET AND IT GLOWS WITH A MOST SPLENDID RED LIGHT. ALLOW THIS LIGHT TO PENETRATE ALL THROUGH THE BASE OF YOUR BODY. FEEL THIS WARM RED GLOW PENETRATE YOUR THIGHS AND ON DOWN TO YOUR KNEES, CALVES, SHINS, AND YOUR ANKLES. FEEL THIS GLOW IN YOUR FEET LIKE A PAIR OF WARM, TOASTY SOCKS. YOU ARE NOW READY TO RECEIVE HIGHER TRANSFORMATION OF ENERGIES, QUICKER AND EASIER RELEASE OF THE OLD, AND HIGHER MANIFESTATION OF YOUR NEEDS AND DESIRES. SIT WITH THIS FEELING FOR AS LONG AS YOU LIKE. GUIDANCE MAY COME NOW OR UNFOLD FOR YOU LATER.

SUMMARY

LESSON 32

What we have discovered about this meditation is that it is very powerful and it is extremely beneficial in maintaining our health on all levels. You will find a variety of feelings and awarenesses happening as your Guardian Angel goes from one center to the next.

We basically experienced the same kinds of feelings doing this lesson. It feels as though your whole body is being revitalized and renewed. A new kind of energy consumes you, and a lightness happens, as your Angel cleans each socket. When you have finished the meditation, you feel like a brand new person.

We have found that sometimes we can sense when one of our bulbs needs to be changed and instead of having to go through the whole exercise, we can just go directly to that one area and have our Angel work on it to clear out whatever is causing the problem, and to put in a new bulb. Many times we even discover the reason or reasons for the problem. For instance, Chris was having a terrible headache one evening and he went into meditation to change that particular lightbulb. As his Angel was working on that area, he received the thoughts which had caused the headache in the first place. He was told to watch his thoughts about that particular situation.

Pat's Guardian Angel, Marshay, told Pat one day that she needed to change her heartlight. She took Marshay's advice and almost immediately started to feel better as the congestion she was having started to clear up.

We have noticed that when our centers are clear and bright, the functions of these centers start to work properly. Our intuition on all levels becomes more accurate. We feel the higher qualities more easily, our visualizations are clearer, we have more success listening to our inner guidance, and we definitely feel healthier.

LESSON 33

REMEMBERING THE MISSION

DO YOU SOMETIMES GET THE FEELING YOU ARE HERE ON A MISSION, BUT FOR THE LIFE OF YOU, CANNOT REMEMBER WHAT THAT MISSION WAS? BEFORE YOU, AS A LIGHT OF GOD, CAME INTO THIS PHYSICAL BODY, YOU HAD THE MEMORY OF ALL OF YOUR PREVIOUS LIFETIMES AND THE LESSONS YOU LEARNED. YOU KNEW WHAT YOU STILL NEEDED TO WORK ON, HOW TO GO ABOUT IT, AND WHO YOU WERE TO DO IT WITH. ALL THIS INFORMATION WAS STORED IN A LOCKET WHICH YOU WORE AROUND YOUR NECK. FOR SOME REASON, WHILE REMOVING YOUR SPIRIT GOWN TO COME NAKED INTO A BODY, YOU LAID YOUR LOCKET ASIDE AND FORGOT TO BRING IT WITH YOU. DOES THIS EXPLAIN WHY MOST OF YOU ARE SO CONFUSED ABOUT YOUR MISSION?

IN LIFETIMES PAST, AFTER STUMBLING ALONG THE BEST YOU COULD, YOU LEFT YOUR BODY AT DEATH AND RETURNED TO RETRIEVE YOUR LOCKET. THEN UPON REVIEWING WHAT YOUR MISSION WAS, YOU SAID, "OH WOW, SO THAT WAS IT!" AND YOU SET ABOUT MAKING PLANS TO TRY AGAIN. THAT WAS WHEN YOU HAD LOTS OF LIFETIMES TO PLAY WITH. AS THINGS SPEED UP NOW, IT BECOMES MORE AND MORE IMPORTANT TO REMEMBER YOUR MISSION AND GET ON WITH IT - NO MORE PIDDLING AROUND! SO WE MUST GO ON A MEDITATIVE JOURNEY BACK TO THE TIME WHEN YOU MISPLACED YOUR LOCKET, FIND IT, AND PUT IT BACK ON TO LEARN TO RETRIEVE THE INFORMATION CONTAINED WITHIN IT.

THE JOURNEY WILL TAKE YOU BACK TO THE MOMENT YOUR PARENTS CONCEIVED THE CELL WHICH WAS TO GROW INTO YOUR PHYSICAL BODY. YOU ARE THERE AT THAT MOMENT TO CLAIM THE BODY IN THE MAKING AS YOURS. YOU DO NOT MOVE INTO IT YET, BUT YOU SORT OF CLAIM IT LIKE AT A BAGGAGE CLAIM AREA AT THE AIR-PORT. AT THIS POINT, YOUR ENERGY CHANGES AS YOU REMOVE THE GOWN AND THE LOCKET. THEN YOU INFUSE THE CELL WITH SOME OF YOUR ENERGY TO HELP THE CELL GROW INTO A BODY ESPECIALLY DESIGNED FOR YOUR MISSION, WHICH YOU HAVE ALREADY FORGOTTEN. THEN YOU SORT-OF HANG AROUND THE DEVELOPING FETUS, VAGUELY RECALLING THAT IT HAS SOMETHING TO DO WITH YOU. THEN AT BIRTH, THE PART OF YOU IN THE BODY DEVELOPS AN ENORMOUS DRAWING POWER. YOU RESIST AT FIRST UNTIL THE DRAW IS SO STRONG THAT YOU JUST POP INTO THE BODY. THE FIRST AWARENESS YOU HAVE IS THE RUDE REMOVAL FROM A WARM, SAFE PLACE TO A COLD, SCARY ONE, AND YOU ARE NOT PLEASED!

SO IN THIS MEDITATION, YOUR GUARDIAN ANGEL WILL FLY YOU BACK TO WHEN THE CONCEPTION TOOK PLACE TO HELP YOU FIND THE LOCKET. NOW SINCE WE ARE USING IMAGINATION, IT IS NOT IMPORTANT HOW YOUR IMAGES CORRELATE WITH ACTUAL FACTS. ALLOW WHATEVER IMAGES THAT COME UP, KNOWING THAT YOU WILL FIND YOUR LOCKET. IT MAY BE IN MOM'S OR DAD'S

HOUSE SLIPPERS, IN A JEWELRY BOX, OR IN A DRESSER DRAWER, OR UNDER AN APPLE TREE. OR IT MAY HAVE FALLEN BEHIND THE SOFA CUSHION, OR IT MAY BE IN THE BACK SEAT OF AN OLD CHEVY. ANYHOW, WHEN YOU FIND YOUR LOCKET, SAY "THANK GOD!" AND IMMEDIATELY PUT IT OVER YOUR HEAD AND AROUND YOUR NECK. THEN COME BACK OUT OF MEDITATION.

NOW I WILL GIVE YOU THE INSTRUCTIONS ON HOW TO USE THE LOCKET TO REMEMBER YOUR MISSION. EVERYONE AND EVERYTHING IN YOUR LIFE IS THERE TO ASSIST YOU IN YOUR MISSION; ACKNOWLEDGING THIS WILL ACTIVATE THE LOCKET. YOU WILL BEGIN REMEMBERING YOUR MISSION WHEN YOU FOCUS ON THE LOCKET, WHILE ASKING, "WHAT IS THE PURPOSE OF THIS IN MY LIFE IN REGARDS TO MY MISSION?" "WHAT IS THIS PERSON HERE TO TEACH ME?" "WHAT DID THAT EX-WIFE OR EX-BOYFRIEND TEACH ME?" "HOW IS THIS JOB PREPARING ME FOR MY MISSION?" IF YOU BECOME STILL, THE ANSWERS MAY COME TO YOU RIGHT AWAY OR YOU MAY GAIN SOME INSIGHTS DURING THE NEXT FEW DAYS. IN TIME, BY CONNECTING PAST EXPERIENCES WITH CURRENT ONES, YOU WILL BECOME CLEAR. THEN DECIDE TO UNDERTAKE THE REST OF YOUR LESSONS AND MISSION WITH LAUGHTER AND LIGHT, FOR YOU KNOW NOW WHY YOU ARE HERE.

SUMMARY

LESSON 33

Sonny asked us to do the meditation part of this lesson that same evening. We had success finding our lockets, but found them in some very strange places.

Booduin took me to the house where I spent the first six years of my life. I searched everywhere that seemed like an obvious place for it to be, but found nothing. Finally, as a last resort, I went out to the garage. I was almost ready to give up when I spotted an old, dirty, rusted toolbox covered with cobwebs. I decided to look inside, only because I was getting desperate, and sure enough - there it was! I didn't get the connection why the locket was there until later. It finally dawned on me that my locket contained all the tools I would need to complete my mission.

Pat had no success searching through the house where she was brought to, which was her grandparents house. She found nothing outside either. She finally decided to go to the barn and search there. Sure enough, she spotted it hanging on a nail near the hay loft. She had to chuckle as she put it around her neck.

Bess eventually found her's under a big cherry tree in the backyard. Cherries are very significant to Bess, because Sonny and Raphael are always comparing her growth to that of a cherry. She has gone from a green, unripe cherry to one which is almost ripe.

Chris searched everywhere for his locket, checking all the not so obvious places first and without success. He finally decided to look in more obvious places and found his locket twisted up in the sheets of his parents' bed. Chris says it is typical of how he sometimes makes his problems more difficult than they really are.

After the meditation was over, we had a lot of laughs sharing our experiences with each other. Those experiences proved to have a special meaning all in themselves. The places and the ways in which we found our lockets gave us valuable insights into our lives.

Our experiences using the lockets have helped us to understand the purpose of certain situations and people who have come into our lives. We do not always get instant answers, but our answers seem to unfold over a period of days. When understanding comes, an acceptance then follows. It also helps with current situations taking place in our lives now. If we can go on the assumption that everything and everyone is part of our mission, then we are able to view whatever is taking place in a whole different perspective.

Pat has been using her locket to help her as she prepares to move. At first she found it extremely difficult to let go of things she has had for many years. She asked her locket about her reluctance. She said it became clear to her that these things had fulfilled a purpose once, but no longer served her now. She was to get on with her life and let the past go. After this realization, she has become ruthless in clearing out what she thought was still important to her.

There are many ways to use the locket, and the more you practice with it, the more ways you will discover. We love learning from our lockets and we are becoming more and more aware of the knowledge and wisdom contained within them.

LESSON 34

CHILDHOOD REVISITED

WOULD IT NOT BE GREAT IF YOU, SOMETIME IN THE FUTURE, DECIDED TO TRAVEL BACK IN TIME TO VISIT YOU TODAY AND GIVE YOURSELF ADVICE, GUIDANCE, LOVE, AND ENCOURAGEMENT? LET ME TELL YOU THAT YOU CAN NOW LEARN A METHOD TO GO BACK TO YOUR CHILDHOOD DAYS, AS YOU ARE NOW, AND VISIT YOURSELF AS A CHILD. DO YOU REMEMBER WHAT YOU LOOKED LIKE, SAY, AT THE AGE OF FIVE, OR SEVEN, OR TEN? MAYBE IT IS TIME TO DIG OUT THOSE OLD SNAPSHOTS, STUDY YOUR FACE AND CLOTHES, AND REMEMBER A SPECIFIC TIME IN YOUR CHILDHOOD WHEN YOU REALLY NEEDED A FRIEND WHO UNDERSTOOD.

THEN IN MEDITATION, SIMPLY GO BACK TO THAT TIME AND MEET YOURSELF AS A CHILD. YOU CAN MEET YOURSELF IN THE BEDROOM, ON THE BEACH, OR IN THE WOODS.

AGAIN, THIS DOES NOT HAVE TO FIT LOGIC OR ACTUAL FACTS, BUT IT IS IMPORTANT THAT YOU FIND A PLACE TO BE ALONE WITH YOURSELF.

WHEN YOU FIRST ARRIVE ON THE SCENE, DO SO QUIETLY WITH A SMILE AND AN OPEN HEART. SAY HELLO TO YOURSELF. YOU, THE CHILD, MAY OR MAY NOT BE STARTLED. TELL YOURSELF, THE CHILD, THAT YOU ARE THEM IN THE FUTURE. ALLOW YOURSELVES TIME TO BE COMFORTABLE WITH EACH OTHER. TELL YOURSELF, THE CHILD, THAT YOU CAME TO BE THEIR FRIEND, AND TO HELP THEM, BY TELLING THEM THINGS THEY WILL EXPERIENCE AS THEY GET OLDER. YOU MAY NOT BE ABLE TO COVER EVERYTHING IN ONE SESSION, SO YOU MAY MAKE MANY VISITS IN THE TIME TO COME. KEEP YOUR INFORMATION TO THE HIGH POINTS AND GOOD STUFF AND GIVE THEM GUIDANCE AND WARNINGS TO HELP THEM AVOID UNNECESSARY PAIN.

WHAT YOU WILL BEGIN TO NOTICE THEN, IN YOUR PRESENT ADULT LIFE, IS THAT MEMORIES OF CHILDHOOD PAINS WILL SUDDENLY BEGIN TO DISAPPEAR, THAT IS IF YOU TAKE YOUR ADVICE. YOU CAN GO BACK AGAIN AND MAKE SURE IF A SPECIFIC PAINFUL EXPERIENCE WAS NECESSARY TO BRING THE CHILD TO CERTAIN PEOPLE OR PLACES. IF NOT, YOU CAN SUGGEST ANOTHER WAY FOR THE CHILD TO HAVE THAT EXPERIENCE. AS MORE OF YOUR CHILDHOOD PAINS DISSOLVE, THE HAPPIER, AND FREER YOU, THE ADULT, WILL BE.

FOR A REAL TREAT, GIVE YOU, THE CHILD, A HUG. HOLD THEM ON YOUR LAP, FEEL THEIR WARMTH, THE SOFTNESS OF THEIR SKIN, AND SMELL THEIR FRAGRANCE. YOU MAY WANT TO PLAY GAMES AND SURPRISE THEM WITH HOW WELL YOU REMEMBER THEIR LITTLE SECRETS.

HAVE A LOT OF FUN AND LAUGHTER WITH YOUR CHILDHOOD SELF, AND REMEMBER THAT EVERY BIT OF LOVE AND UNDERSTANDING YOU GIVE THE CHILD TRANSLATES INTO A BETTER YOU, THE ADULT.

SUMMARY

LESSON 34

Working with our child-selves has been so rewarding and has given us so many insights into ourselves. It opened up so many buried memories and helped us to really see where some of our insecurities came from. It helped us get in touch with the many freedoms our child-selves enjoyed, like the freedom to dream, play, discover, and to really enjoy life to the fullest. You know, all of those things we forget to do as adults. But by watching our child-selves play, it helped us realize just how important it is to continue being that free child.

My child had no fears of me at all the first time I visited her. While she played in the woods, I just stood there and watched her for the longest time before I approached her. She was so busy running around doing this or that and playing with her doll. She eventually discovered an ant hill and stopped to watch the activity, and that is when I made myself known to her. She was not afraid of me, but full of so many questions. When she discovered who I was, she asked even more questions. She seemed to accept who I was, but I am not sure she really understood. I think I was just another game to her. Since our first visit, I have gone back to visit her many times. She has told me some of her problems and we are working on them together.

It took Pat several times to finally talk to her child. Pat was puzzled at first, not understanding why her child kept running away from her. Then she remembered how her parents had instilled in her not to talk to strangers. Finally after her child had seen her enough times, Pat was able to talk with her. Pat tried to explain who she was to the child, but the child didn't really grasp it. She kept asking Pat, "How can you be me in the future when the future isn't here yet?" Pat just couldn't get the little girl to understand. Pat told the child that she would have a happy childhood and a wonderful life. But she did warn the child about a certain man who would come into her life, who would not be good for her, and told the little girl not to marry this man. Pat continues to visit the child and they are becoming buddies.

Chris met his child right after a traumatic experience. The little boy had just broken a fruit jar over his little brother's head. He was hiding up in an apple tree, scared to death he would be punished. Chris appeared in the tree beside him. The first thing Chris did was surround the little boy with an energy of peace and love and assure him that everything would be alright. The little boy told Chris that he was glad he had come again. This surprised Chris and he asked the little boy what he meant by again. The little Chris replied, "I met you on the school bus my first day of school, and you told me that school was fun and that the nuns weren't as scary as I thought. And you were right." Chris thought about that, and came to the conclusion that, even when we aren't aware, portions of ourselves must cross over into other dimensions. This experience has helped Chris get through other apparent traumas more easily.

Bess has been carrying around with her some very painful events from her childhood, and going to visit her child has been significant in helping her process this out. She has been helping her child deal with all of the guilt and fear of these experiences and trying to instill trust into the little girl again. Bess says her child needs reassurance that she is loved. She has been noticing some changes recently in the child, in that she is happier and more fun loving.

We really have noticed a change in ourselves from working with our kids. The more love and understanding we give to them, the more we notice our own insecurities lessening. It is a special feeling to give our kids those things we thought we were deprived of. I know the more we continue to do for them, the better we are going to feel.

LESSON 35

THE TRYING TEENS REVISITED

DIG OUT YOUR OLD YEARBOOKS AND TEEN-AGE PHOTOS. LOOK AT THAT HAIR, AND THOSE BRACES AND THOSE HORN RIM GLASSES. YOUR TEENS WERE WHEN YOU WERE PLANNING YOUR FUTURE AND DEVELOPING ALL OF THOSE FEARS, PHOBIAS, AND IDENTITY PROBLEMS YOU CARRIED INTO YOUR ADULTHOOD. THERE WERE PROBABLY MANY SIGNIFICANT THINGS, WHICH YOU EXPERIENCED, THAT HELPED SHAPE YOU. THERE WERE ALSO MANY TIMES WHEN YOU NEEDED ENCOURAGEMENT TO GO ON AND DO THE RIGHT THINGS. THESE ARE THE TIMES WHEN YOU MIGHT BENEFIT MOST FROM GOING BACK IN MEDITATION TO VISIT YOURSELF AS A TRYING TEEN.

HERE YOU MAY FIND A MOST UNWILLING SUBJECT ON WHOM TO TOSS PEARLS OF WISDOM. ALL A TEEN NEEDS IS ONE MORE ADULT GIVING ADVICE. HERE IS WHERE YOUR

SKILL WITH THE LOCKET WILL COME IN HANDY. YOU CAN TELL THEM HOW THIS CLASS REALLY HAD IMPORTANT STUFF YOU NEEDED LATER ON; AND HOW THAT PERSON REALLY BECAME A FRIEND IN NEED OR A FRIEND IN DEED. YOU CAN SHOW THEM A SLICE OF THE BIG PICTURE, AND TELL THEM THE REASONS FOR THIS OR THAT. THEY MAY LOOK AT YOU LIKE YOU ARE CRAZY AND IT MAY NOT SINK IN, BUT YOU LAID THE GROUNDWORK. WHEN THOSE EVENTS AND PEOPLE DO COME UP, THEY WILL RECALL YOUR WORDS AND IT WILL MAKE A DIFFERENCE FURTHER DOWN THE ROAD INTO ADULTHOOD. THE ENCOURAGEMENT YOU GIVE THEM, AS WELL AS THE ACCEPTANCE OF WHO THEY ARE WILL HAVE AN AFFECT ON YOUR LIFE YEARS LATER. ANY JOKE YOU TELL THEM WILL THRILL THEM. COMPLIMENTS WILL GO A LONG WAY IN HELPING THE TEEN DEVELOP CONFIDENCE AND A POSITIVE SELF-IMAGE. HOW CAN THIS NOT HELP YOU OUT LATER ON?

COMFORT IS IMPORTANT WHEN YOUR TEEN'S HEART IS BROKEN. HE/SHE NEEDS TO KNOW THAT THERE IS LIFE AFTER REJECTION. AND SO WHAT IF YOU WERE NOT PICKED FOR THE TEAM, THIS LEFT YOU FREE TO EXPERIENCE ALL OF THE OTHER NEAT STUFF YOU CAN TELL YOUR TEEN ABOUT. AND SO WHAT IF YOU GOT INTO SOME KIND OF TROUBLE? IT DOESN'T MATTER, YOU LOVE THEM TO PIECES ANYWAY. YOUR SON/DAUGHTER GREW UP JUST FINE, AND HECK, YOU GOT OUT ON PAROLE IN JUST A FEW MONTHS.

HAVE SOME FUN WITH THIS AND HAVE SOME LAUGHS WITH YOUR TRYING TEEN. YOU WILL BE SURPRISED AT WHAT GREAT UNDERSTANDING YOU DEVELOP BY REMEMBERING HOW YOU FELT, WHAT YOU WORRIED ABOUT, WHAT MATTERED TO YOU AND WHAT WAS GOING ON IN YOUR HOME, SCHOOL, AND IN OTHER ACTIVITIES. ADULTS CAN GAIN SIGNIFICANT AWARENESS ABOUT THEIR LIVES JUST BY REVISITING THEIR TRYING TEEN SELF.

SUMMARY

LESSON 35

Working with our teens is helping us deal with other types of problems our child-selves hadn't been exposed to. As Sonny stated in the lesson, problems dealing with self-image, identity, and rejection are teenage problems that affect us, as adults, unless we look at them and solve them.

I went to visit my teen on a beach. She always went there alone to think about all the things she couldn't talk to anyone else about. I remember even then, she used to wonder about life and why people in the world acted the way they did. She didn't understand the hatred, the prejudice, or the cruelty people would inflict upon one another. She used to ask God about it, along with many other deep subjects she continually thought about. I knew I would have a tough job ahead of me, because even today, I don't know all the answers. But it turned out better than I expected. All she wanted was to talk to someone who would understand her concerns and confusions. She told me how she would sneak out of her bedroom at night to go down to the beach and talk with God. I go and meet her there often. Recently she told me she was reluctant to grow up and become one of the 'so called' adults who confused her so. Booduin, my Guardian Angel, recently explained to me her reluctance. I have been trying to help her understand some of what I have just been told. She understands more than I thought she would. I really enjoy all of our talks and discussions and we are both benefiting from them.

Pat went back to a time in her teen's life just after the break-up of an important relationship. Her teen was sitting in a park swing looking very sad. After explaining who she was, Pat tried to explain to the teen why this had happened. She told the teen that one day in the future, this boy would re-enter her life. That got the teen's attention and led to numerous questions. Pat answered as honestly as she could. She told the teen that soon she would meet another man who would father a little girl for her. That really excited her teen, but Pat went on to explain that this relationship would not last very long and not to be too upset by it because it had to break-up in order for her to meet the love of her life. As Pat did with the child, she also warned the teen about the man who was not good for her. The teen was interested in all of this, but her main concern was this boy who had just broken her heart. Pat tried to tell her it would be years into the future, but she and the boy would eventually meet up again. Knowing that she would see this boy again helped her teen deal better with the pain she was experiencing. Pat says her teen was really well adjusted, except for this one big heartbreak. She wants to rekindle some of the joy, the spark of adventure and spontaneity her teen had, and to learn how to have more fun again. She feels her teen can help her do all of this.

Bess' teen was difficult to reach. It took several visits before her teen would open up enough for Bess to talk with her. Eventually, her teen started to trust Bess and told her some of her insecurities and fears. Bess grew up in a less fortunate family, which made it hard for her to feel accepted. She tried hard to always look her best hoping it would give her the acceptance she needed. She felt that if she didn't look just 'perfect' she would be teased and judged. Bess realized she needed to help her teen with self-confidence, self-worth, and to help her teen see her own specialness. Bess started by explaining that her life was likened to an apple and they would start together peeling off the skin, (which the adult Bess doesn't like anyway!) Bess told her it would be like peeling off her own self-imposed shell which covers the sweet, unique person who hides underneath it. As Bess continues to work with her teen, she is gaining more self-confidence in herself as an adult and she isn't looking outside of herself for approval as often. She is learning, too, that it is not her outside appearance which is important, but who she is on the inside that really matters. Working with her teen has helped Bess see her own special uniqueness and to appreciate who she is.

Chris says the biggest problem his teen encountered was finding his own unique identity and feeling good about who he was. Chris decided to visit his teen as a counselor first, instead of telling him who he really was. He said his teen may not be open to the truth until he gained his teen's trust. He said he would tell him eventually as the teen's sessions progressed. The teen trusted Chris, as a counselor, much more quickly than Chris had anticipated. He told Chris how he would adopt the mannerisms and clothing of whatever group he was with at the time, and how confusing it was for him. The teen was confused because he didn't know who he really was. Chris counseled his teen by suggesting that maybe he was merely sampling some of the many identities before settling on just one which was truly his own. He told the teen that by sampling all of these identities, he would soon start to discern what felt right to him and what did not. The teen now is aware of who Chris really is and both of them are working together on discovering their own unique identity. They are both working on discerning what feels right to them, and discovering what a major stepping stone it is in their spiritual growth.

So you see, working with your teen can be very liberating. We have found it to be extremely important in our growth and in helping us bring to the surface hidden impediments to that growth. As Sonny once said, "*LOOK DEEP, AND LIKE A GOOD DISH WASHER, SCOUR THE CRUD OUT.*" Working with our teen has certainly helped us to find some of that crud!

LESSON 36

REWRITING YOUR PAST

DO YOU EVER WISH YOUR LIFE HAD BEEN DIFFERENT? DO YOU FEEL THAT IF YOUR PAST HAD BEEN DIFFERENT, YOUR LIFE TODAY WOULD BE BETTER AND YOU WOULD BE HAPPIER? HAVE YOU EVER WISHED YOU COULD CHANGE CERTAIN EVENTS IN YOUR LIFE? AND WHAT ABOUT SOME OF THE DECISIONS YOU HAVE MADE, DO YOU WISH YOU COULD GO BACK AND CHANGE SOME OF THEM? WHAT ABOUT YOUR FAMILY LIFE? DO YOU WISH IT WOULD HAVE BEEN DIFFERENT? DO YOU SOMETIMES BLAME YOUR PAST FOR SOME OF THE FAILURES AND THE PROBLEMS YOU HAVE TODAY?

IF YOU HAD THE OPPORTUNITY TO GO BACK IN YOUR PAST AND CHANGE EVERYTHING YOU WANTED, WOULD YOU? WELL, I AM HERE TO TELL YOU THAT IT IS INDEED POSSIBLE TO DO JUST THAT. SINCE EVERYTHING IS HAPPENING CONCURRENTLY, IT MEANS THE PAST IS STILL

ALIVE AND HAPPENING RIGHT NOW. SO YOU HAVE THE POWER TO CHANGE WHAT YOU THINK OF AS YOUR PAST. YOU CAN CHANGE IT TO WHATEVER YOU WANT IT TO BE. FOR INSTANCE, LET US SAY YOUR FATHER DIED OR LEFT HOME WHEN YOU WERE YOUNG AND YOU HAVE ALWAYS WISHED HE HAD BEEN THERE. YOU CAN CHANGE THAT. AND WHAT ABOUT YOUR MOTHER, WAS SHE ALWAYS TOO BUSY WITH HER OWN LIFE THAT SHE HAD LITTLE TIME FOR YOU? YOU CAN ALSO CHANGE THAT. THE EVENTS IN YOUR LIFE CAN BE CHANGED AS WELL. THAT PAINFUL EVENT DID NOT TAKE PLACE AND THAT WONDERFUL EXPERIENCE YOU WANTED TO HAPPEN REALLY DID HAPPEN. YOU CAN CHANGE YOUR PAST TO BE WHAT YOU WISHED IT HAD BEEN.

THIS LESSON, THEN, IS TO SIT DOWN AND REALLY THINK ABOUT YOUR PAST. WHAT WOULD YOU LIKE TO CHANGE? ALSO, THINK ABOUT HOW DIFFERENT YOUR LIFE WOULD BE TODAY HAD YOUR PAST BEEN DIFFERENT. AFTER YOU ARE FINISHED WITH ALL OF THIS, I WANT YOU TO ACTUALLY WRITE YOUR NEW PAST DOWN ON PAPER. START WITH YOUR CHILDHOOD AND MOVE UP TO THE MOST RECENT PAST. WHEN YOU HAVE FINISHED, READ IT OVER AND REALIZE THAT YOU ARE DIFFERENT NOW BECAUSE OF THIS NEW PAST.

YOU WILL SOON DISCOVER MANY OF YOUR FEARS, HANG-UPS, EXCUSES, AND 'REASONS WHY NOT' WILL SIMPLY START TO FADE AWAY. AFTER ALL, YOUR PAST IS DIFFERENT AND SO ARE YOU.

IT IS CRUCIAL YOU DO THIS EXERCISE SOON, SO YOU CAN BEGIN TO LIVE THE LIFE YOU HAVE ALWAYS WANTED AND RICHLY DESERVE. HOW HAVE YOU CHANGED NOW THAT YOUR PAST IS DIFFERENT? THIS LESSON, WHEN DONE HONESTLY AND EARNESTLY, WILL HAVE A POWERFUL AFFECT UPON YOUR FUTURE. SO LET US BEGIN NOW TO UNDO THAT OLD PAST AND CREATE A MOST MARVELLOUS NEW YOU!

SUMMARY

LESSON 36

'Rewriting Your Past' is remarkable in it's effectiveness to produce amazing results. It was a surprise to all of us how quickly this lesson works.

Approximately ten years ago, I made a snap decision in my life I came to regret almost immediately. This decision created for me an incredible amount of guilt, shame, and feelings of unworthiness beyond words. I felt I did not deserve anything good life had to offer. I continually punished myself for making that decision. I could not forgive myself, no matter how hard I tried. I tried many techniques, meditations, and even sought help from many healers in hopes that they could help me with all the pain I was feeling, but to no avail. The pain was too deep and the guilt too strong. I continually sabotaged any happiness which presented itself to me. But after rewriting my past and changing that decision, I can honestly tell you I feel no pain. It is truly a miracle! I can't emphasize to you enough how this lesson has changed my life.

Pat's main focus, when rewriting her past, was her most recent past. Pat was having trouble letting go of material things she considered important. She rewrote her past to say that she did not get attached to material things and how easy it was for her to discard them. It worked, and now as she prepares to move, she has no difficulty in selling or giving these things away. She is amazed at the change in her attitude.

Chris wrote about both his distant past and recent past. His focus was on relationships which had caused him pain. He changed all the fights and disagreements of these relationships and instead created understanding and patience. The break-ups that occurred in these relationships were no longer painful, but now harmonious and mutual. He focused on his negative feelings toward these relationships. For instance, the blame he harbored after a painful relationship no longer existed in his new past, nor did the projection of old relationships onto new ones occur. Pain just did not exist as he rewrote his past. He also went through and changed all of the unfavorable ways he had handled interpersonal conflicts with his family and co-workers. The results have simply amazed him. As he puts it, "The results have made me a wonderful guy!" (As his wife, I will have to agree with him. He really is a wonderful guy!) Chris is now more comfortable with himself and others. His whole attitude about life has changed.

Bess wrote about her life in general and grouped many of her decisions and experiences in a more generalized way. For instance, she wrote that she had never intentionally hurt anyone and that she was always there for her children, etc. She did, however, focus on her more recent past and has changed some of her decisions. She says her life is now changing with surprising results. She feels not only is it hard to remember her old past, but is now feeling all of the higher qualities she has always wanted to feel. She says lesson 26, "The Qualities Of Being There", is easier for her to do now as a result of doing this lesson.

What happens when you rewrite your past is that the memories, if you can even remember them, no longer push your buttons. You lose your emotional attachment to those events. Chris likened it to taking off dirty clothes you have worn too long. We recommend you do not procrastinate doing this lesson, because the results are profound and the growth so astounding. Remember, too, if you forget to change something, or if you discover more later you would like to change, you can. It dosen't have to be done all at once.

LESSON 37

FUTURE SELF COMES TO VISIT
or
THE OLD GEEZER DROPS BY FOR A CHAT

HAVE YOU EVER WONDERED WHAT THE FUTURE HOLDS FOR YOU, AND MAYBE WHAT YOU WILL LOOK LIKE IN FIVE, TEN, OR TWENTY YEARS? EXCLUSIVELY AVAILABLE TO YOU IN THE PRIVACY OF YOUR OWN HOME, IS SONNY'S 'INVITE YOUR FUTURE SELF KIT' THAT YOU MAKE YOURSELF. THE FIRST THING YOU NEED TO GET IS A LOVELY GREETING CARD WHICH SAYS WHAT YOU WOULD LIKE TO SAY TO YOUR FUTURE SELF. YES, THERE ARE SOME CARDS THAT WERE NOT MEANT FOR THIS OCCASION, BUT WILL BE MOST APPROPRIATE. BE SURE TO ADDRESS THE CARD TO YOUR FUTURE SELF, LIKE "SUSAN IN TEN YEARS" AND SIGN IT "SUSAN IN DECEMBER 1990". NEXT YOU WILL NEED A TALL, LIT CANDLE IN A HOLDER. YOU WILL NEED A TABLE

ON WHICH TO PLACE THE CARD AND CANDLE, AND A COMFORTABLE PLACE TO SIT (PEACEFUL MUSIC IS OPTIONAL).

NOW SHUT OFF ALL OF THE LIGHTS. UNPLUG THE PHONE, AND READ ALOUD THE CARD. THEN STATE ALOUD, "I DESIRE TO HAVE MY FUTURE SELF IN (HOWEVER MANY) YEARS VISIT ME." NOW GAZE INTO THE CANDLE FLAME, THINKING ABOUT SEEING YOUR FUTURE SELF. AFTER AWHILE, IF YOU HAVE A STILL MIND, YOU WILL ENTER INTO A LIGHT TRANCE AND START SEEING A FACE, YOUR FUTURE SELF, IN OR AROUND THE FLAME. THIS REALLY IS A PROJECTED IMAGE OF AND FROM YOUR FUTURE SELF. SAY "HI" TO YOURSELF, AND WHATEVER ELSE COMES TO YOU. YOU WILL HEAR WORDS BACK FROM YOUR FUTURE SELF. IT MAY HAVE ADVICE FOR YOU OR A COMPASSIONATE EAR, OR YOU CAN PLAY QUESTION AND ANSWER. SOME OF THE BEST QUESTIONS YOU CAN ASK ARE ONES LIKE, "WHAT CAN I DO NOW THAT WOULD MAKE THINGS BETTER FOR ME LATER?" "WHAT IS THE BEST WAY TO RESOLVE THIS PROBLEM IN MY LIFE?" WRITE DOWN ALL OF THE INFORMATION YOU GET, EVEN IF IT SEEMS TO MAKE NO SENSE, FOR IT MAY LATER ON. IF YOU DO NOT SEE AN IMAGE OF YOUR FUTURE SELF OF SO MANY YEARS, START OVER AND INVITE YOUR FUTURE SELF OF A FEW YEARS SOONER. THEN GIVE YOURSELF THE 'A' SIGN (Fonzie's thumbs up sign) AND YOUR FUTURE SELF WILL DO IT BACK. REALIZE THAT EVERYTHING YOU DO FOR YOUR GROWTH FROM NOW ON WILL BENEFIT THAT WONDERFUL LIGHT OF GOD YOU SAW IN THE CANDLE FLAME.

SUMMARY

LESSON 37

We all got very excited after we received this lesson from Sonny. We couldn't wait to get started on it. We weren't successful with our first attempts, though. Unexpected problems came up.

Bess' first attempt didn't work. Her second attempt produced for her what Sonny calls her own little light show, but she did not see anything nor receive a message. I did not see anything but a small green light that flickered. Pat and Chris both procrastinated even doing the lesson. Chris wasn't sure why he hesitated, but Pat said she had fears that she would not see anything. We asked Sonny to give us some insights into why we were not successful with this lesson. "*YOUR DIFFICULTIES WITH MEETING THE OLD GEEZER IS BOTH FEAR OF WHAT THE FUTURE HOLDS AND WHAT IT MAY NOT HOLD. YOU ARE AFRAID TO SEE THAT MAYBE THE RESULT OF YOUR PROCRASTINATION NOW, WILL SPELL MISSED OPPORTUNITIES AND SHATTERED DREAMS IN THE FUTURE. AND YOU ARE CORRECT. NOT ONLY DOES EVERYTHING YOU DO NOW AFFECT YOUR FUTURE, BUT EVERYTHING YOU DO NOT DO AS WELL. SO, AS YOU TAKE ACTION ON YOUR DREAMS, YOU WILL BE MORE EXCITED ABOUT SEEING YOUR FUTURE SELF. ALSO, THE MAIN PURPOSE OF VISITING YOUR CHILD AND TEEN IS TO HELP THEM OVER THE ROUGH SPOTS, THEREBY ERASING SOME OF THE PAIN AND HURTS FROM YOUR PAST AND TO GIVE YOU A CLEARER EMOTIONAL AND PERSONAL WORK SPACE IN WHICH TO MAKE YOUR DESSERT OF THE FUTURE. THE OLD GEEZER'S PURPOSE IS TO DO THE SAME FOR YOU.*"

After Sonny's message, we all had to do some honest soul-searching about what he had said. We had to admit we all had some of those fears still inside of us. We worked on processing out these fears and took steps to ensure the fulfillment of our dreams. Just before we were going to attempt it again, Sonny gave us another helpful technique. "*FOR THOSE STRUGGLING WITH THE FUTURE SELF, TRY THIS PLEASE. PUT A MIRROR ON THE OTHER SIDE OF THE CANDLE FACING YOU. WHILE FOCUSING ON THE CANDLE, YOU SHOULD AT LEAST SEE A FACE OVER THERE LOOKING BACK. AS YOU CONTINUE TO FOCUS ON THE CANDLE, THE IMAGE OF YOUR FUTURE SELF WILL BEGIN TO TAKE FORM IN THE MIRROR REFLECTION. TRY IT.*" Our next attempts were more successful.

Bess started out by telling her future self up front that she was not afraid of what she would see because she knew if she did not like it, she had the power to change it. She then started to focus on the candle and quiet her mind. This is what happened. The room became bathed in a brilliant light, so white that it was almost blue. She heard a ringing or hum, which she refers to as a spirit connection. There was a very soft spirit presence in front of her. It was still and seemed gentle and peaceful. She then asked to see her future self of one year and asked that she be told what she could do now to make her future better. She was just using the candle and did not see a face, but saw and felt a presence. She started then to receive this message: "Continue to practice the lessons and become a master at them. Work on your gifts. Have certainty of purpose. For now, be content. It will all unfold." She also received some future stuff she is waiting to see unfold.

Chris, being the artist that he is, decided to make his own greeting card to give to his future self which said exactly what he wanted it to say. He started then to focus on his future self of five years. He saw, briefly, a small face in the heart of the candle flame. He was more aware of an energy or presence sitting across from him. This presence spoke to him telepathically in Chris' own voice. His message consisted of advice and helpful suggestions to help him make his future better. Here is a portion of that message. "It has been quite some time since I've even thought about how things were in 1991. One thing I would like to impart to you is this: realize that in whatever situation you find yourself, it is only there for the moment in which you formulated that perception. Every moment offers you the opportunity to change your perception of any given situation. The situation, itself, may not change. What will change is your viewpoint, what it means to you, how it affects you, and how you are going to deal with it. Accepting this truth, grants you the power to overcome any obstacle. One more thing I wish I would have done when I was your age is to develop a burning desire to produce paintings and get them shown. I would also take better care of my health. I would rarely be found in front of the tube, except for special evenings to watch a movie with Susan." Chris has already started taking this advice and he is having positive results.

My second attempt proved more successful as well. I decided to use the mirror, as Sonny suggested. I asked to see my future self of one year. At first, I saw only my reflection as I look now, but as I gazed into the mirror, the face changed. It looked more at ease and I must say, somewhat younger. The stress seemed to disappear. She was smiling at me and gave me this message which I, also, received in my head. "My main message to you is not to get discouraged. Keep taking Sonny and Booduin's advice. Do not let little disappointments cause you such worry. Believe me, you will soon realize that worry only prolongs any situation that you face. You will come to really understand this truth very soon. You are just weeks away from a brand new life." She went on to tell me what was coming up for me, if I could just let go of the worry.

Pat had the most successful experience of all. After gazing intently into the candle, a face appeared. It remained there, with it's mouth actually moving, while Pat received her message. This is what her future self told her. "Deny not your heritage. You were born to live in freedom with joy and love. Love of yourself, as you are, makes the love of you by others inevitable. And the love you give to others is a gift that will bring you great joy, and the joy of giving is the gift that will bring freedom into your life. Your life is going to hold more rewards in it than you could ever imagine. Keep showing your light." Pat said after this experience, she went to look at herself in the mirror, and like my experience, the face she saw in the candle was younger looking than the face she saw staring back at her in the mirror. Pat was puzzled by this.

As you can see, we all had rather unique experiences. We will continue to practice this lesson, because we know how helpful it can be for our futures. We want our futures to be the best we can make them and we will follow any suggestions given to us to insure that they will be. Do not be discouraged if you have trouble at first with this lesson. Just keep practicing and processing out all of the fears which might be blocking your success. With determination, you will succeed.

LESSON 38

DEVELOPING A STILL MIND

ONE OF THE MOST VALUABLE SKILLS YOU WILL EVER USE IN YOUR SPIRITUAL GROWTH IS 'FOCUS'. THE LETTERS STAND FOR: FILTERING OUT COMPLETELY USELESS STUFF. *'FOCUS' CREATES A STILL MIND. WITH A STILL MIND, YOU ARE MUCH MORE ABLE TO RECEIVE GUIDANCE. WITH A STILL MIND, YOU ARE ABLE TO TUNE INTO AN ISSUE OR PROBLEM AND FIND SOLUTIONS MUCH MORE QUICKLY THAN BEFORE. YOU HAVE SO MANY THOUGHTS GOING THROUGH YOUR MIND ALL DAY LONG, IT IS NO WONDER THAT YOU HAVE CONFUSION AND DIFFICULTY PICKING OUT THE PEARLS FROM THE HOG SLOP. YOUR MIND IS LIKE A RADIO THAT CAN RECEIVE MANY STATIONS AT ONCE, AND THAT IS BOTH DISTURBING AND USELESS TO THE SEEKER OF ONE CLEAR STATION. YOUR RADIO HAS A TUNING DIAL TO PULL IN ONLY ONE STATION AT A TIME. ARE YOU PULL-*

ING IN AN FM (FOUL MESSAGE) OR AN AM (ANGEL MESSAGE) STATION? WHEN YOU DEVELOP A STILL MIND, IT IS LIKE ADDING A TUNING DIAL CALLED 'FOCUS' TO YOUR MENTAL RECEIVER.

WITH 'FOCUS', YOU WILL BE ABLE TO SHAVE YEARS OFF YOUR PATH OF STRUGGLE AND CONFUSION AND SPEED YOURSELF ALONG THE PATH OF EASE AND CLARITY. A VERY SIMPLE EXERCISE TO DEVELOP A STILL MIND IS TO FOCUS YOUR ATTENTION ON A FLOWER, PREFERABLY A SINGLE BLOOM, ON A SINGLE STEM, IN A SIMPLE VASE. NO MULTIPLE BLOOMS OR GREEN STUFF! THEN YOU SIT COMFORTABLY IN FRONT OF THE FLOWER AND STUDY THE BLOOM, THE WHOLE BLOOM, AND NOTHING BUT THE BLOOM. IF YOUR THOUGHTS WANDER, SIMPLY BRING YOUR ATTENTION BACK TO THE BLOOM. YOU MAY GET OFF TRACK A LOT AT FIRST, BUT PLEASE PERSEVERE. YOU WILL SOON BE ABLE TO HOLD YOUR CONCENTRATION FOR LONGER AND LONGER PERIODS OF TIME. AFTER YOU THINK YOU ARE PRETTY GOOD AT IT, CLOSE YOUR EYES AND RECREATE THE BLOOM IN YOUR MIND. THEN OPEN YOUR EYES AND COMPARE THEM. THEN STUDY THE BLOOM AGAIN, WITH FOCUS AND CONCENTRATION. THEN CLOSE YOUR EYES AND RECREATE THE BLOOM UNTIL YOU FEEL AS IF YOU COULD NOT TELL THE REAL BLOOM FROM THE IMAGE BLOOM. THIS MAY SOUND BORING, BUT IT IS EXCITING TO THINK ABOUT ALL OF THE BENEFITS OF A STILL MIND. AFTER EVEN MINIMAL SUCCESS, YOU WILL NOTICE A DRAMATIC IMPROVEMENT IN YOUR ABILITY TO RECEIVE GUIDANCE AND INSIGHTS, AND YOU MAY BE VERY PLEASED TO SEE HOW THIS IMPROVES YOUR VISUALIZATION SKILLS. 'FOCUS' ON!!

SUMMARY

LESSON 38

We are still working on developing our still minds. We found it more difficult than we realized. We found visualizing the bloom the easiest part, but trying to quiet our minds is another story. We hadn't realized just how hard it would be to concentrate on one thing for any length of time. It takes great discipline. The constant chatter that went on within our minds, when we thought we had it well under control, was an eye-opener. We realized just how little control we have over the thoughts which go through our minds.

After a few weeks trying to develop our still minds, we became rather frustrated. One evening we decided to ask Sonny why we were having so much trouble with this lesson. This was his comment to us: "*RELAX AND TAKE IT LIGHTER, FOR THE TASK IS TO CREATE THE STILL MIND, NOT THE SERIOUS MIND.*" We had to admit we had gotten much too serious trying to do this lesson, and that alone was contributing to our frustration. Since then, I have discovered a little trick that works for me. When other thoughts creep in, I just say "cancel, cancel", and immediately the thought is gone.

It has gotten easier for us the more we have practiced. Pat's visualization skills have improved and we have had some success with getting insights and solutions. There is still more work to do in getting this lesson mastered. We have had the most success when we do this lesson in a calm, peaceful mood to begin with. We are working now towards developing a still mind at times when we feel anxious or stressful, and we will continue to practice until we are able to easily quiet our minds whenever we need to.

LESSON 39

GO TELL IT ON THE MOUNTAIN

BY THIS TIME, YOU HAVE MADE SOME CHANGES AND DECISIONS. YOU HAVE CREATED, AND YOU KNOW WHAT ELSE YOU WANT. NOW IS THE TIME TO AFFIRM EVERYTHING; SHOW GRATITUDE; STATE YOUR PURPOSE; AND TO HAVE EVERYONE YOU KNOW, AND THE REST OF THE WORLD, AFFIRM IT AND WANT IT FOR YOU. NOW IS THE TIME TO GO TELL IT ON THE MOUNTAIN.

THIS IS A MEDITATION, BUT FIRST WRITE A FEW THINGS DOWN THAT YOU WANT TO AFFIRM - LIKE ABUNDANCE; THEN A FEW THINGS YOU WANT - LIKE A NEW JOB; THEN SOMETHING YOU ARE GRATEFUL FOR - LIKE YOUR GOOD FRIENDS. THEN IN YOUR MEDITATION, YOU FIND A BEAUTIFUL LITTLE CREATURE AT THE BASE OF A TALL MOUNTAIN. IT COULD BE A MOUNTAIN GOAT, OR A BEAR CUB, OR AN ANGEL, OR WHATEVER APPEARS THERE. THIS CREATURE

WILL GUIDE YOU TO THE TOP OF THE MOUNTAIN. FOLLOW IT ON THE TRAIL, WHICH UNFOLDS BEFORE YOU. MAKE IT A REAL JOURNEY. SEE THE TREES AND ROCKS AND FERNS. SMELL THE FOLIAGE. HEAR THE SOUNDS. SUDDENLY YOU FIND YOURSELF AT THE TOP OF THE MOUNTAIN. YOU LOOK DOWN AND IT SEEMS LIKE THE ENTIRE WORLD IS BELOW YOU. THERE IS YOUR FAMILY AND FRIENDS AND PEOPLE YOU HARDLY KNOW. THEY ARE ALL LOOKING UP AT YOU. YOU SHOUT "HELLO". THEY SHOUT BACK. YOU FEEL THEIR LOVE. THEN YOU SHOUT YOUR AFFIRMATION, "I HAVE ABUNDANCE!" THEY SHOUT BACK, "YES, YOU HAVE ABUNDANCE!" YOU SHOUT, "I WANT THIS NEW JOB." THEY SHOUT BACK, "IT IS YOURS, GO FOR IT!" YOU SHOUT, "I AM GRATEFUL FOR MY GOOD FRIENDS." THEY SHOUT BACK, "YOU DESERVE THEM AND YOU HAVE MANY MORE." DO THIS A FEW MORE TIMES WITH A FEW MORE THINGS. REALLY FEEL THE CROWD'S ENERGY, LET THEIR WORDS SINK IN. HAVE FUN, THEN THANK THEM ALL AND COME OUT OF MEDITATION.

SUMMARY

LESSON 39

This beautiful meditation has a way of making you feel like anything is possible. You feel so powerful and full of energy; almost like you are full of adrenalin and it's radiating out from you in all directions.

Looking down and seeing all of those people looking up at you, and wanting for you what you want, gives you a tremendous sense of awe. When you hear them all shouting and affirming, supporting all that you want, it is a wondrous feeling. It helps you affirm the support of the universe. It gives you a feeling that you cannot fail.

We have all had similar experiences with this lesson. Successes have happened for each of us. We have found that using other lessons, along with this one, helps in bringing results even more quickly. Here are some of the other lessons we have used: #14 - If You Can Think Of It, You Can Create It; #17 - I Get By With A Little Help From My Friends; #26 - The Qualities Of Being There Are The Vehicles To Get You There; #29 - Going For The Essence. I am sure there are many more that you will discover, also, to use with this lesson.

After doing this lesson, notice how positive and alive you feel. It is a great way to affirm to yourself and to the universe that you mean business! If you are still in that place where you feel you need permission to have what you want, then this lesson is an excellent way to get that permission. All of those people are saying YES, YES, YES to you!

LESSON 40

PLANETARY TRANSFORMATION

HAVE YOU EVER NOTICED HOW NEGATIVE THE NEWS IS, ALL FULL OF CONFLICT AND SCARCITY? I TELL YOU, SOME DAYS OUR HANDS ARE REALLY FULL. ANGELS ARE HERE TO ASSIST IN PLANETARY TRANSFORMATION.

ONE GREAT WAY YOU CAN HELP US, IS TO PERSONALLY BROADCAST LOVING THOUGHTS OF PEACE AND ABUNDANCE. YOUR THOUGHTS HAVE AN INCREDIBLE AMOUNT OF POWER TO TRANSFORM NEGATIVE ENERGY INTO POSITIVE ENERGY. ONE LOVING, POSITIVE THOUGHT CAN CANCEL OUT THOUSANDS OF NEGATIVE THOUGHTS. TRY HAVING LOVING THOUGHTS ABOUT YOURSELF AND NOTICE HOW PEOPLE RESPOND TO YOU DIFFERENTLY.

A FUN AND POWERFUL MEDITATION IS TO IMAGINE YOURSELF FLOATING OUT IN SPACE, HIGH ABOVE THE EARTH. FROM YOUR VANTAGE POINT, BEGIN TO BROAD-

CAST LOVING, PEACEFUL THOUGHTS. SEE OR IMAGINE YOUR THOUGHTS, LIKE RADIO WAVES, ENTERING THE EARTH'S ATMOSPHERE AND ENTERING PEOPLE'S HEARTS. KNOW THAT YOUR POSITIVE, LOVING THOUGHTS ARE GOING TO WHERE THEY ARE MOST NEEDED TO CANCEL OUT THOUGHTS OF HATRED, ANGER, PREJUDICE, SCARCITY, AND WAR.

BACK ON EARTH, YOU CAN AVOID THE NEWS COMPLETELY AND STILL LIVE A FULFILLED LIFE. ALSO, WHEN YOU HEAR PEOPLE SAYING NEGATIVE THINGS, YOU CAN SILENTLY THINK OF SOMETHING NICE LIKE CHILDREN SMILING, ANGELS SINGING, FLOWERS BLOOMING, OR THAT FUNNY THING YOUR CAT DID. BY DOING THESE THINGS, YOU HELP THE ANGELS BRING ABOUT PLANETARY TRANSFORMATION.

ON BEHALF OF ALL ANGELS, I THANK YOU FOR YOUR LIGHT, YOUR LOVE, AND YOUR HELP.

SUMMARY

LESSON 40

This lesson has been very exciting and we have had wonderful results with it. Knowing too, that we are helping the Angels with our own planet's transformation, makes this lesson extra special. It is easy to do and takes very little time. We have noticed, when working with people, that they do respond in a positive way to us when we are having loving thoughts about ourselves. When we have loving thoughts about others, the same positive results occur.

Chris has really noticed the results of this lesson, particularly with a certain co-worker. This person, on a daily basis, arrives at work complaining about this or that. It used to affect Chris, either causing him to feel depressed, or causing him to feel irritated. Chris would respond to his co-worker's complaining by agreeing with him, or saying something like, "Gee, that's too bad", which would reinforce this persons negativity. Lately, however, Chris has been practicing this lesson with his co-worker by thinking positive, happy thoughts, and also saying aloud to this person, light and happy responses. It helps Chris counteract not only his own negative feelings about the situation, but also helps his co-worker see the lighter side of his situation. Now this person only complains once or twice a week.

Pat has had a similar experience with one of the ladies she volunteers with at the hospital. This lady never had a smile on her face, nor did she ever have anything nice to say. Pat called her a real grump. Pat decided to try this lesson out on her. It worked, and now the lady smiles at Pat and seems much happier.

Bess notices all kinds of responses from people, some that even surprise her. The young people that are around her on a daily basis are more responsive and even openly affectionate.

She gets warmer hugs now! She has noticed complete strangers approaching her with huge smiles on their faces and her first thought is, "Do I know you from somewhere?" Then she realizes that it is her new state of mind which has caused this. It helps Bess be more aware of all the inward changes that have taken place within her. She can openly see it manifesting in her physical reality.

My experiences with people have been very similar to the others. We all see the results quickly and the results have always been positive.

The planetary exercise is a wonderful exercise and feels so powerful when you are doing it. The results, however, are not as easy to see, as with the people you are directly involved with. We do this on a consistent basis with the conflicts in the world. We do this lesson, along with lesson 31 - "Playing With Light".

We all want to do everything we can to help with our planet's transformation and to help with the personal transformation of all of us who share this planet.

QUESTIONS AND ANSWERS

FROM SONNY

Q How did Angels originate?

A *GOD CHUCKLED AND OUT THEY POPPED. WE WERE BORN OUT OF A DESIRE FOR THE 'ALL THAT IS' TO KNOW ITSELF IN A MULTITUDE OF WAYS. CREATION IS! WOULD YOU LIKE THAT STUCK ON YOU BUMPER? CREATION IS! CLEVER IS IT NOT?*

Q How do Angels get their names?

A *A NAME IS A VIBRATION. A VIBRATION SOMETIMES BEGETS A SOUND WHICH TRANSLATES INTO A NAME - SUCH AS THE SOUND OF BOODUIN. SOME OF US ARE NAMED BY THE ELDER ANGELS. SOME ADOPT A NAME FROM A PERSON'S SUBCONSCIOUS. SOME ARE NAMED BY GOD.*

Q Do Angels wear clothes?

A *IN ALL MY YEARS OF ANGELING, I HAVE YET TO SEE A NAKED ANGEL. WHEN THEY APPEAR TO PEOPLE, THEY ARE TASTEFULLY ATTIRED IN ANGEL GARB, OR THEY HOP INTO TRADITIONAL CLOTHING OF THE PREVAILING CULTURE WHERE THEY ARE. IN OUR NATURAL STATE, HOWEVER, AS A BEING OF LIGHT, CLOTHES ARE ENTIRELY UNNECESSARY. WOULD YOU COVER A LIGHT BULB WITH A PAIR OF BOXER SHORTS?*

Q What do Angels look like?

A *WE ARE PRIMARILY LIGHTS OF GOD. SOME HAVE BEEN KNOWN TO MATERIALIZE. YOU HAVE ALL SEEN SOME AND MAY NOT HAVE KNOWN IT. SOME LOOK LIKE REGULAR FOLKS, AS THIS BIBLE VERSE ILLUSTRATES: HEBREWS 13, SECOND VERSE; "DO NOT FORGET TO BE KIND TO STRANGERS, FOR SOME WHO HAVE DONE THIS HAVE ENTERTAINED ANGELS WITHOUT REALIZING IT". SOME HAVE FLAIR AND SPORT WINGS. I HAVE FLAIR! IF I WERE TO COME INTO A PHYSICAL BODY, I WOULD LIKE TO LOOK LIKE CHRIS' DRAWINGS, BUT BIGGER. WE DO NOT, I REPEAT, DO NOT, HAVE HALOS STICKING IN US, PERIOD!*

Q Do human beings, after death, have a choice to become an Angel?

A *LET ME CHECK WITH MICHAEL LANDON. ANGELS SOMETIMES CHOOSE TO BE BORN INTO HUMAN BODIES. PEOPLE, AFTER DEATH, CAN WORK AND COMMUNICATE AS SPIRIT. BUT AN ANGEL IS A SEPARATE BEING THAT HUMANS DO NOT HAVE THE CHOICE TO BECOME. A TREE CAN BECOME LUMBER, BUT LUMBER CANNOT BECOME A TREE.*

Q What is it like where you are from?

A *A. LIKE THE BACK SEAT OF A FIFTY-EIGHT CHEVY. THERE IS ALWAYS A PARTY GOING ON. THERE IS AN ABUNDANCE OF FUN, LOVE, JOY, CHEVYS, AND LIGHT. IT IS LIKE RIDING ON A RAINBOW, AND THERE IS ALWAYS GOD'S LOVE SHINING ON US.*

Q Is this how you would describe Heaven?

A *THIS IS ANGELTOWN. HEAVEN IS ANYWHERE THAT YOU ARE OPEN TO GOD'S LOVE.*

Q Is there anyone besides God that you report to?

A *REPORT TO? LET ME CHECK. NOBODY THERE!*

Q Do you ever take a vacation? And if so, what do you do?

A *I HANG OUT AT THE SEVEN-ELEVEN AND WATCH THAT THING THAT GOES AROUND WITH THE WIENERS. ACTUALLY, VACATIONS ARE FOR THOSE WHO WORK, AND I PLAY ALL THE TIME.*

Q Are you with us even when we are not having our sessions?

A *THERE ARE MANY WITH YOU ALWAYS. YOU ARE ENJOYING THE FEELING OF NEVER BEING ALONE. I AM OFTEN WITH YOU, ESPECIALLY WHEN YOU THINK OF ME, HOWEVER, I DO NOT WATCH OVER YOU, SO TO SPEAK. MY FUNCTION IS MORE THAT OF A GUIDE AND MESSENGER.*

Q Are there such things as 'Dark Angels'?

A *ANGELS ARE OF THE LIGHT. GOD DID NOT CREATE ANYTHING BAD. ONLY FEARFUL AND NEGATIVE PEOPLE COULD EVEN THINK OF SUCH THINGS. EVIL IS ONLY IN THE MINDS OF HUMANS. THERE WAS NEVER ANY FALL OF LUCIFER AND THERE WAS NEVER A DEVIL, NOR IS THERE A HELL. THESE BIZARRE MYTHS WERE CREATED BY HUMANS, NOT GOD. STORIES OF BAD THINGS ARE WORTHLESS TO*

THE SPIRITUALLY EVOLVED, AND BESIDES, THEY HAVE NO HAPPY ENDINGS. ALL GOOD STORIES HAVE HAPPY ENDINGS.

Q If you had to calculate your age in years, how old would you be?

A *IF I WERE TO CALCULATE MY AGE IN YEARS, I WOULD BE TWENTY- NINE, GIVE OR TAKE A FEW THOUSAND YEARS.*

Q What do you do when you are not dictating to us?

A *WELL, I DO NOT JUST SIT AROUND ON MY ANGEL BUNS AND PLAY A HARP. IN ADDITION TO OBSERVING HUMANS, THERE ARE ALL SORTS OF ANGEL CONFERENCES TO ATTEND, AS WELL AS OUR SESSIONS OF LIGHT WITH GOD. I ALSO GO SLIDING DOWN RAINBOWS, AND PERIODICALLY, WE HAVE A ROUSING GAME OF TAG. SOME DAYS THOUGH, IT TAKES ALL OF OUR TIME TO ILLUMINATE JUST A SMALL PART OF YOUR MINDS. CAN YOU SAY STUBBORN?*

Q Would you ever want to become human? And if so, why?

A *KNOWING WHAT I KNOW, IT WOULD BE FUN. I WOULD, OF COURSE, WANT TO EXPERIENCE BOTH MALE AND FEMALE BODIES. I WOULD LIKE TO BE AN INFANT, AND A CHILD, AND A VERY OLD GEEZER. I WOULD LIKE TO HAVE A BABY; TO BAKE PIES; RUN; AND COMB MY LUSCIOUS RED HAIR. I WOULD LIKE TO MAKE LOVE, THEN FALL ASLEEP. I WOULD LIKE TO HAVE A BEER AND I WOULD LIKE TO RIDE A MOTORCYCLE. IF I WAS TO BE ANYONE IN PARTICULAR, I WOULD BE FONZIE. I LIKE THE WAY HE SNAPS HIS FINGERS AND THE JUKE BOX PLAYS.*

Q What is it you find most interesting about us humans, and what is the most difficult to understand?

A *YOUR INCREDIBLE RANGE OF EMOTIONS; YOUR INCREDIBLE RANGE OF EMOTIONS.*

Q Do you feel other emotions besides love?

A *WHAT OTHER EMOTION IS THERE? LOVE COVERS ALL.*

Q What is the most important thing that we as humans need to understand?

A *I WOULD HAVE TO SAY THE 'TEN REMINDERS' GOD GAVE ME TO DELIVER TO YOU.*

Q Why is it that we don't remember what we chose to learn in our lifetime?

A *WHY DO PEOPLE FORGET THEIR GLASSES, THEIR CAR KEYS, THEIR SHOPPING LISTS? LACK OF FOCUS. NOT IN THE PRESENT TIME. THE MORE YOU EVOLVE, THE MORE YOU REMEMBER. YOU NEVER DID LEAVE THE LIGHT, YOU JUST STARTED BELIEVING IN THE ILLUSION THAT YOU ARE SEPARATE FROM GOD, AND YOU MUST BE SLOWLY RE-PROGRAMED BACK TO REALITY. WHY NOT ALL AT ONCE, YOU ASK? IF I WERE TO TELL YOU THAT YOU ARE GOD, HOW FAR WOULD I GET IN REALLY CONVINCING YOU THAT WAS TRUE?*

Q Are our Guardian Angels assigned to us or do they choose us?

A *IT IS NEITHER. IT IS DIFFICULT TO EXPLAIN, BUT GOD SAID THAT EACH SOUL WAS TO HAVE A GUAR-*

DIAN ANGEL TO ACCOMPANY IT THROUGHOUT IT'S EXISTENCE, AND SO IT WAS, AND IT WAS GOOD. THERE WAS NO CHOOSING NOR ASSIGNING. YOUR GUARDIAN ANGEL IS WITH YOU FROM THE VERY FIRST INCARNATION UNTIL YOU, AND YOUR ANGEL, MERGE TOTALLY INTO THE LIGHT - MEANING BACK TO GOD TOTALLY FOR KEEPS. I, HOWEVER, NOT BEING A GUARDIAN ANGEL, CHOSE YOU, AND IT WAS GOOD.

Q Do animals have Guardian Angels?

A *YES, ANIMALS HAVE GAURDIAN ANGELS. THEY ARE DIFFERENT FROM HUMAN ANGELS IN THAT THEIR SPECIALTY IS ANIMALS. THEY ASSIST THE ANIMAL'S SPIRIT IN CHOOSING THE LIFETIMES IT IS BORN INTO, AND THE KIND OF ANIMAL IT WILL BE, HOW AND WHAT PACE IT WOULD EVOLVE, AND TO SOME EXTENT, WHETHER OR NOT IT WILL INTERACT WITH HUMANS. FOR INSTANCE, AN ANIMAL SPIRIT MAY DECIDE THAT IT HAS LEARNED ENOUGH ABOUT BEING A SQUIRREL SO THE ANGEL PREPARES IT TO BECOME A CAT OR A DOLPHIN OR A BLUEJAY. ANIMALS DO INCARNATE MORE THAN ONCE. SOMETIMES AN ANIMAL WILL CHOOSE TO BE WITH THEIR FORMER MASTER AGAIN. SKYE WAS ONCE A CUTE LITTLE DOG NAMED MUFFIN.* (Skye is our cat and Muffin was a dog I once had.)

Q Our Guardian Angels have male or female names, how is that determined?

A *ANGELS ARE, YOU MIGHT SAY, BEYOND CLASSIFICATION OF GENDER. IT IS HUMANS WHO SEE US AS MALE OR FEMALE BASED ON WHAT OUR NAMES SOUND LIKE TO THEM. A NAME IS A VIBRATION. EACH PERSON'S TRAIL OF LIFETIMES HAS A THEME AND CERTAIN VIBRATIONS JUST FIT CERTAIN THEMES. THIS IS THE EXPLANATION OF GUARDIAN*

ANGELS. FOR OTHER ANGELS, SUCH AS 'YOURS TRULY', THE VIBRATION OF THE NAME FITS THE THEME OF WHAT WE ARE HERE TO DO. MY NAME FOR INSTANCE, WHILE BEING A TERM OF ENDEARMENT, WAS GIVEN TO ME BY THE ELDER ANGELS, TO SIGNIFY THAT I WAS BROUGHT INTO ANGELHOOD MUCH LATER THAN THEY. I COULD HAVE BEEN CALLED JUNIOR, OR KID, OR RUNT, OR SQUIRT, BUT WITH THE MISSION THAT WAS GIVEN ME BY GOD, SONNY HAS THE ONLY SUITABLE VIBRATION FOR ONE WHO BRINGS SO MUCH SUN AND LIGHT INTO PEOPLE'S LIVES. WE DO, HOWEVER, REFER TO EACH OTHER AS HE OR SHE SIMPLY BECAUSE IT IS MORE MARVELLOUS TO THE HUMAN EAR THAN IF WE CALLED EACH OTHER THAT OR IT.

Q Are there other Angels, besides our Guardian Angel, who are with us throughout our lifetimes?

A *OODLES TO BE SURE. IT IS NOT EVEN A COMPREHENSIBLE NUMBER. SOME ANGELS WITH SPECIFIC ROLES TO PLAY IN YOUR LIFE COME TO THE FOREGROUND FOR A SHORT TIME, SOME FOR MOST OF YOUR LIFE, BUT MOST DO THEIR WORK SUBTLY IN THE BACKGROUND. THERE IS A LOT OF OVERLAPPING. ALSO, SOME ANGELS MAY WORK WITH OVER A MILLION PEOPLE AT A TIME.*

Q Why is it that some Angels can appear to people and others cannot?

A *TO APPEAR IN HUMAN FORM, AN ANGEL MUST STEP DOWN THEIR ENERGY A GREAT DEAL, AND THERE NEEDS TO BE A HIGHER ENERGY SOURCE, SUCH AS CRYSTALS. IT ALSO TAKES GREAT SKILL TO TAKE ON THE DENSER ENERGIES OF THE EARTH PLANE. MOST OF US EXIST AS LIGHT ONLY, HOWEVER, IT IS A LIGHT TOO BRIGHT TO SEE WITH YOUR PHYSICAL*

EYES. WE CAN, HOWEVER, PLAY WITH CLOUDS, AND SUNLIGHT, AND CANDLE FLAMES, AND TOUCH YOU GENTLY.

Q What happens after total enlightenment?

A *AFTER ENLIGHTENMENT, AND THE TOTAL MERGING INTO THE LIGHT, THERE WILL BE A MYRIAD OF OPTIONS FOR EXPRESSION, WHICH OF COURSE, I COULD NOT BEGIN TO EXPLAIN AND YOU, OF COURSE, WOULD NOT HAVE THE SLIGHTEST INKLING AS TO WHAT THE DEUCE I WAS YAPPING ABOUT.*

Q Where did God come from, and was there actually a beginning?

A *GOD ALWAYS WAS. YOU CAN SAY THAT GOD IS HIS OWN BEGINNING.*

Q 1. What is your mother's maiden name?
2. When is your birthday?
3. What is your social security number?
4. Will you ever sign on this account?

(The reason for these questions is because they were asked to me by a bank teller. Sonny asked me to open a savings account for him at this particular bank, and when asked these questions, I was at a loss as to how to answer them. I am sure the bank teller thought I was a nut, because of the way I reacted to her questions, and I was caught off guard. I acted quite strangely, to say the least!)

A *MY MOM'S MAIDEN NAME WAS GODDESS. SHE HAD A COSMIC UNION WITH DAD, GOD THE FATHER, AND THEY BECAME 'ALL THAT IS'. AS FAR AS A DATE OF BIRTH GOES, THERE WERE NO CALENDARS AROUND.*

I HAVE EXISTED AS AN ANGEL EVER SINCE MY FIRST AWARENESS OF MYSELF. I DO NOT HAVE A SOCIAL SECURITY NUMBER, BUT I AM A MEMBER OF THE ANGELIC ASSISTANCE ASSOCIATION, OR TRIPLE A. AND IT IS TRUE THAT I CAN NOT SIGN MY NAME, BUT I DID LEAVE MY MARK ON YOU. (I decided against calling the teller with this information.)

Q Are you in the room with us when we aren't having our sessions?

A *I AM ALWAYS IN THE ROOM WITH YOU. I KIND OF FLOAT AROUND. ON MY LEVEL OF AWARENESS, ALL PLACES ARE HERE. YOU SEE, TIME AND SPACE ARE ILLUSIONS AND I CAN EXPERIENCE ANY PORTION OF THE ILLUSIONS FROM ANY PLACE, WHICH IS NOT A PLACE, ANYWAY.*

Q Do our Guardian Angels and Higher Selves help God answer prayers?

A *GOD ALWAYS ACTS THROUGH HIS MANY HELPERS.*

Q Will your book be a major factor in helping people become totally enlightened?

A *YES, BRINGING THE CONCEPTS OF ANGELS AND HIGHER SELVES TO PEOPLE IS ONE OF THE MAJOR CONTRIBUTIONS WHICH WILL ASSIST IN THE ENLIGHTENMENT OF THE HUMAN RACE.*

Q Do Angels have significant others?

A *WE DO NOT HAVE SIGNIFICANT OTHERS, UNLESS ALL ARE CONSIDERED. YOU SEE, PEOPLE TAKE EXCLUSIVE PARTNERS BECAUSE THEY ARE NOT CAPABLE OF LOVING THEMSELVES FULLY OR REAL-*

LY MORE THAN ONE OTHER AT A TIME. THEY PAIR FOR REASONS LIKE CHILD PRODUCTION, TO KEEP FROM BEING LONELY, OR TO SHARE CERTAIN LESSONS AND GROWTH. WE DO NOT HAVE ANY OF THESE DRIVES OR MOTIVATIONS, AND WE LOVE OURSELVES FULLY AND ALL OTHERS EQUALLY. WE NEVER FEEL LESS THAN WHOLE AND CONNECTED AND NEVER SEPARATE OR ALONE. AND WE ALWAYS FEEL TOTALLY LOVED AND ACCEPTED BY ALL OTHER ANGELS. NEAT, HUH?

Q When we partner in a relationship, do each others' Guardian Angels work together to enhance the relationship?

A *EACH AND EVERY PERSON ONE IS PARTNERED WITH, WHETHER ONE TERMS IT FOR BETTER OR WORSE, IS FOR ONE'S GROWTH AND LIFE ENHANCEMENT. WHETHER OR NOT ONE GETS FROM THE PARTNERSHIP WHAT ONE IS SUPPOSE TO IS DEPENDENT ON HOW WELL ONE LISTENS TO AND FOLLOWS ONE'S ANGEL'S GUIDANCE. I WILL SAY ALSO THAT THERE HAS YET TO BE A RELATIONSHIP FORMED THAT AN ANGEL DID NOT HAVE A HAND IN.*

Q Why do we sometimes find ourselves dealing with the same issues over and over again?

A *IT IS YOU WHO PLACE OBSTACLES IN YOUR PATH TO BE YOUR TEACHERS. THE INTENT IS TO RECOGNIZE WHEN THE TEACHER COMES INTO THE CLASSROOM, SO YOU CAN SIT UP STRAIGHT AND LISTEN, IN ORDER TO UNDERSTAND THE LESSON AND MOVE AHEAD. IF, HOWEVER, YOU GET CAUGHT SHOOTING SPIT BALLS OR SLEEPING IN CLASS, THEN THE TEACHER WILL BOX YOUR EARS, MAKE YOU WEAR A DUNCE CAP, AND STAND YOU IN THE CORNER, AND THEN YOU WILL HAVE TO TAKE THE WHOLE CLASS OVER. YOU SEE, LIFE IS LIKE A SERIES OF SPIRALS, SOME BIG,*

SOME SMALL, WHERE AT VARYING INTERVALS, SITUATIONS, LESSONS, AND EVEN PEOPLE, KEEP RETURNING TO YOUR CLASSROOM OF LIFE. THAT IS WHY SOMETIMES YOU FIND YOURSELF SAYING, "I THOUGHT I DEALT WITH THIS ALREADY." BUT YOU SEE, THERE IS A DIFFERENCE BETWEEN DEALING WITH BY UNDERSTANDING A LESSON AND DEALING WITH BY JUST HOLDING ON UNTIL YOUR SPIRAL TURNS. YOU MAY KEEP RUNNING INTO THAT PLACE WHERE YOUR BELIEFS ARE TESTED. WHEN YOU ARE JUST DEALING WITH BY HOLDING ON, THINGS MAY SEEM FINE FOR AWHILE UNTIL YOUR SPIRAL HITS THAT PLACE AGAIN. THEN IT WILL KNOCK YOU FOR A LOOP. BUT IF YOU TRULY MASTER THE LESSON BEING PRESENTED, YOU WILL QUICKLY SKIP THROUGH IT. AGAIN, I REMIND YOU THAT YOUR PRESENT REALITY REFLECTS, OH SO CLEARLY, WHAT YOUR THOUGHTS AND BELIEFS ARE.

Q Is there intelligent life, as we know it, on other planets? If so, do the Angels we know travel and visit there also?

A *YES, BUT NOT AS YOU KNOW IT. MANY OF THOSE TERMED 'ALIEN' ARE ACTUALLY FOLKS FROM HERE WHO HAVE SLIPPED, EITHER ACCIDENTLY OR WITH PURPOSE, THROUGH A SORT OF TIME OR DIMENSIONAL WALL. OFTEN THEY ARE JUST AS SHOCKED AS THE PEOPLE WHO SIGHT THEM. MANY UFO'S ARE IN THE MIND. ANGELS HERE DO NOT TRAVEL TO OTHER PLANETS, NOR DO ANGELS THERE TRAVEL HERE. PENGUINS DO NOT VISIT THE OSTRICH AND FISH DO NOT VISIT BEETLES.*

Q What are the differences between Angels, Elves, and Fairies?

A *THEY ARE DIFFERENT CATEGORIES OF GOD'S HELPERS WITH DIFFERENT TASKS. WHILE ANGELS ARE PRIMARILY OF THE SPIRITUAL REALM AND WORK WITH THE SPIRITUAL EVOLVEMENT OF HUMANS;*

FAIRIES ARE MORE CLOSELY CONNECTED WITH THE PLANET AND IN PARTICULAR WITH THE WORLD OF PLANTS. ELVES, I BELIEVE, BAKE CRACKERS AND COOKIES.

Q What is God really like?

A *GOD IS MY BUDDY, MY BEST FRIEND. GOD RADIATES TOTAL LOVE AND ACCEPTANCE. GOD IS NOT THE SLIGHTEST BIT JUDGMENTAL - PEOPLE ARE. UNFORTUNATELY, DUE TO THE LACK OF PROPER PERCEPTION OF GOD, PEOPLE MADE GOD IN THEIR IMAGE. GOD DOES NOT PUNISH - PEOPLE DO. GOD SEES ONLY OUR PERFECTION, FOR THAT IS WHAT HE CREATED. GOD DOES NOT CREATE BAD THINGS - PEOPLE DO. GOD CONSTANTLY SHOWERS LOVE ON ALL CREATION. PEOPLE HAVE TROUBLE ACCEPTING LOVE. GOD DOES NOT MAKE TERRIBLE THINGS HAPPEN. IT IS UP TO EACH OF YOU TO LEARN HOW TO MAKE YOUR OWN HEAVEN OR HELL. GOD DOES NOT INTERFERE WITH YOUR FREE WILL TO DO SO . THIS WAS GOD'S AGREEMENT WITH YOU WHEN YOU FIRST SPLIT OFF FROM* **ALL THAT IS**, *AS A LIGHT OF GOD, TO GO FORTH AND EXPRESS YOURSELF IN A MULTITUDE OF WAYS. THINGS SEEM THE WAY THAT YOU PERCEIVE THEM, BECAUSE YOU FORGOT YOUR MISSION AND THE BIG PICTURE. PEOPLE HAVE MADE GOD INTO ALL SORTS OF THINGS, TO CONTROL OTHER PEOPLE AND GAIN POWER, AND JUSTIFY THEIR ACTIONS OR SHORT COMINGS. "OH, BUT IT WAS GOD'S WILL." GOD IS NOT TO BE FEARED. PEOPLE WHO SAY THEY ARE GOD- FEARING MISS OUT ON THE BEST PART OF GOD - GOD'S LOVE AND GENTLENESS. THOSE WHO SAY YOU NEED TO SUFFER OR DEVOTE YOURSELF TO A STRICT REGIME IN ORDER TO BE IN GOD'S FAVOR, PREACH BALONEY! LIFE IS MEANT TO BE LIVED FULLY. I TELL YOU THAT WHEN STRICT RELIGIOUS FANATICS LEAVE THEIR BODIES AND SEE THE TRUTH OF WHAT THEIR LIVES COULD HAVE BEEN LIKE, THEY ARE OFTEN MOST ASTONISHED. IS GOD AN OLD MAN WHO SITS ON A*

THRONE? SOME PERCEIVE GOD THAT WAY, OR A YOUNG MAN OR WOMAN, OR A BRIGHT LIGHT, OR A DOVE. WE HAD ONE FELLA CROSS OVER LAST WEEK WHO SAW GOD AS A RUEBEN SANDWICH. YOU SEE, HE DID NOT BELIEVE IN GOD AND RUEBENS WERE THE LAST THING ON HIS MIND. I BELIEVE HE RAN A DELI. GOD IS EVERYTHING MADE BY GOD. WHAT GOD DID NOT MAKE DOES NOT EXIST. ALL THINGS WE PERCEIVE AS BAD ARE MERELY ILLUSIONS, AND SOME PEOPLE REALLY BELIEVE IN THEIR ILLUSIONS. I SEE GOD AS A BIG, CUDDLY BEAR OF A MAN WHO IS ALWAYS MOST PLEASED TO HAVE ME CLIMB ONTO HIS LAP. YOU SEE, THE HIGHEST QUALITIES YOU COULD EVER IMAGINE CAN BE ATTRIBUTED TO GOD AND YOU WOULD STILL ONLY GLIMPSE A SMIDGEN OF GOD'S TOTAL ESSENCE. YOU MAY HAVE HEARD GOD DESCRIBED AS ALL KNOWING, ALL SEEING, AND ALL POWERFUL. GOD IS, BUT GOD GETS A KICK OUT OF HOW MUCH THIS SOUNDS LIKE SUPERMAN. WE ALL GOT HIM A RED CAPE LAST YEAR FOR A LAUGH. HE LOVED IT! DOES GOD ANSWER YOUR PRAYERS? GOD KNEW ALL YOUR PRAYERS LONG BEFORE YOU WERE CREATED, AND OF COURSE GOD'S ANSWER TO ALL PRAYERS IS YES! YOU JUST NEED TO BELIEVE IT TO BE SO. MY BUDDY, GOD, IS ALSO YOUR BUDDY AND WANTS SO MUCH FOR YOU ALL TO OPEN TO HIS LOVE AND TAKE TO HEART HIS 'TEN REMINDERS' AND LET HIM BE YOUR BEST FRIEND, TOO.

Q You have turned out to be, in many ways, very different from our previously held conceptions of what Angels were like. Can you explain this?

A *YOU MEAN, WHY DID I NOT SHOW UP BIGGER THAN LIFE, QUOTING BIBLE VERSES AND SWINGING A SWORD TO BATTLE THE FORCES OF EVIL? I UNDERSTAND THAT THIS IS THE IMAGE OF ANGELS YOU HAVE BEEN GIVEN THROUGH OLD PAINTINGS, SCULPTURES, AND STORIES. THESE IMAGES ARE*

LARGELY SYMBOLIC TO CONVEY PERSONAL OR COMMONLY HELD MYTHS AND BELIEFS. YOUR REALITY, WHAT IS 'REAL' TO YOU, IS AN OUTWARD EXPRESSION OF YOUR INNERMOST THOUGHTS AND BELIEFS. APPARENTLY, YOU COULD NOT RELATE TO, BELIEVE IN, OR FEEL COMFORTABLE WITH A STRICT AND JUDGMENTAL SWORD SWINGING ANGEL. I THEN, FILLED A DESIRE IN YOU FOR A WARM, LOVING, LIGHT, AND FUNNY ANGEL. YOUR BELIEFS SAID THAT AN ANGEL COULD BE FRIENDLY, APPROACHABLE, AND A BUDDY, MUCH LIKE I AM SHOWN IN THIS BOOK'S ILLUSTRATIONS. I AM A VERY UNIQUE AND SPECIAL BEING. I WILL ALSO BE EXPERIENCED DIFFERENTLY BY EACH PERSON BECAUSE OF THEIR VARIOUS BELIEFS.

QUOTES AND INSIGHTS

BY SONNY

- *EACH TIME YOU BRING SOME TYPE OF JOY INTO ANOTHER'S LIFE, YOU ARE DOING GOD'S WORK.*
- *INTEREST AND TRUST MUST WORK TOGETHER TO PRODUCE THE BEST RESULTS.*
- *SAYING SOMETHING NICE, ESPECIALLY TO SOMEONE YOU FIND DIFFICULT TO LIKE, HEALS A DOZEN WOUNDS.*
- *LOOK FOR THE LIGHT IN ALL PEOPLE AND YOUR WAY WILL BE WELL LIT.*
- *IT IS MOST DIFFICULT TO MAKE A GIANT LEAP WITH SHORT LEGS. SEVERAL SMALLER STEPS WILL GET YOU TO THE SAME PLACE.*
- *TAKE THOSE THINGS THAT REALLY BUG YOU AND FIND SOMETHING TOTALLY RIDICULOUS AND FUNNY ABOUT THEM, THEN LAUGH YOURSELF HEALED. ENLIGHTENED FOLKS ARE KNOWN FOR THIS TRICK.*
- *GIVE JOY TO THE WORLD EACH DAY AND NOTICE IT CHANGE.*
- *IT IS NOT THE PLACE THAT MAKES YOU HAPPY, BUT THE HAPPINESS YOU BRING TO THE PLACE.*

- *NOTHING SHOULD BE TAKEN SERIOUSLY, EXCEPT DESSERT.*

- *PEOPLE ARE LIKE TIRES. SOMETIMES THEY PERFORM BETTER WITH A LITTLE PRESSURE. TOO MUCH AND THEY POP!*

- *CONFUCIUS ANGEL SAY: ONE CANNOT GET AT THE DELECTABLE MEAT OF A WALNUT UNTIL ONE CRACKS SHELL.*

- *CONFUCIUS ANGEL SAY: FOOL SITS IN MUD AND COMPLAINS; WISE ONE MAKES FINE HOME OF MUD BRICKS.*

- *CONFUCIUS ANGEL SAY: IN ORDER TO LEAVE FOOTPRINTS, ONE MUST TAKE STEPS.*

- *IS THERE ANYTHING AT ALL THAT CANNOT BE POSSIBLE WITH BELIEF?*

- *CONFUCIUS ANGEL SAY: PERSON WITH LIFE CLUTTERED, HAS NO ROOM FOR ENLIGHTENMENT.*

- *TO FEEL GOOD EVERYDAY, START WITH THESE WORDS: SOON SOMETHING WONDERFUL IS GOING TO HAPPEN. THEN LOOK FOR IT.*

- *PRACTICE GIVING MORE OF WHAT COSTS NOTHING, LIKE LOVE, JOY, HAPPINESS, HUGS, SMILES, ETC., AND ALL WILL PROSPER.*

- *ANGELS BECKON YOU TO ACKNOWLEDGE THEM AND THEY EAGERLY AWAIT THE CHANCE TO WORK AND PLAY WITH YOU.*

- *DO NOT LIMIT YOURSELF BY BUYING INTO THE BELIEF THAT YOU CANNOT MAKE A LIVING DOING WHAT YOU LOVE.*

- *THE LORD GIVETH TO THOSE THAT GROWETH.*

- *CONFUCIUS ANGEL SAY: CHOPSTICK NOT TO BE EATEN, BUT TO EAT WITH. ONE MUST KNOW A TOOL FROM A NON-TOOL.*

- *ATTACHMENTS TO YOUR ILLUSIONS, ESPECIALLY THOSE WHICH SERVE NO PURPOSE, STUNT YOUR GROWTH. THE FREER AND SIMPLER YOUR LIFE, THE EASIER IT IS FOR ENLIGHTENMENT TO VISIT. FOR THE WORD ITSELF INVOLVES LIGHTENING UP. GOOD STUFF, HUH?*

- *WHICH EXCITES YOU MORE? WALKING DOWN A WELL TROD PATH THAT YOU KNOW, OR BLAZING YOUR OWN TRAIL THROUGH UNCHARTED WOODS TO WHERE YOU KNOW NOT, OR STROLLING DOWN A SELDOM USED LANE WHICH CAN LEAD ANYWHERE YOU WANT IT TO? THE MORAL IS: WELL TROD PATHS ARE FOR DULL, BORING FOLKS WITH NO IMAGINATION AND NO SENSE OF ADVENTURE. THE WOODS ARE FOR BEARS AND FOOLS, WHILE THE SELDOM USED LANE IS FOR SPECIAL INDIVIDUALS WITH IMAGINATION AND DREAMS, SEEKING TO FULFILL THOSE DREAMS WITH FUN, JOY, LOVE, LIGHT, ADVENTURE, AND LAUGHTER.*

- *LIFE TAKES FUNNY TURNS SOMETIMES AND THE EVOLVED PERSON MAKES THE MOST OF ANY TURN.*

- *A NEW GOLDEN RULE FOR YOU: WHERE IT WAS ONCE, "DO UNTO OTHERS AS YOU WOULD HAVE OTHERS DO UNTO YOU", NOW IT IS, "WANT AND WISH FOR OTHERS WHAT YOU WANT AND WISH FOR YOURSELF."*

- *THERE IS ONE THING THAT REALLY BUGS ME, AND THAT IS WHEN PEOPLE DRAW ANGELS WITH HALOS. IT WOULD BE SO UNCOMFORTABLE IF WE WORE THEM. WE CERTAINLY WOULD NOT BE AS HAPPY AS WE ARE IF WE HAD THOSE STICKING IN US!*

- *WHY WOULD ONE WITH SO MUCH TO GIVE, HIDE THEIR LIGHT UNDER A BUSHEL BASKET?*

- *REMEMBER TO JUDGE NOT WHERE OTHERS ARE. OBSERVE THE SIMILARITIES RATHER THAN THE DIFFERENCES BETWEEN YOU.*

- *CONFUCIUS ANGEL SAY: ONE CANNOT FEAST ON HARVEST FROM GARDEN UNTIL ONE FIRST PLANTS SEED AND WAITS.*

- *CONFUCIUS ANGEL SAY: ONE WHO WAITS FOR COCONUT TO FALL FROM TREE EVENTUALLY GETS WISH, IF COCONUT NOT FALL ON HEAD.*

POEMS

BY SONNY

ANGELS IN THE BATHROOM
ANGELS IN THE SKY
ANGELS IN THE KITCHEN
EATING APPLE PIE

ANGELS WEAR DISGUISES
LIKE BUMBLE BEES AND ANTS
ANGELS CAN BE ANYONE
IN SKIRTS OR SHORTS OR PANTS

ANGELS ARE CORNY
ANGELS ARE FUN
ANGELS HAVE SOMETHING
FOR EVERYONE

ANGELS GET NOT TIRED
THEY WORK ALL DAY AND NIGHT
TO HELP YOU GROW
AND MAKE YOU LAUGH
AND GUIDE YOU TO THE LIGHT

ANGELS COME WHEN NEEDED
WE COME IN A WINK OF AN EYE
WE ALL WANT TO BE THERE
WHEN YOU HAVE YOUR CHERRY PIE

JOKES
BY SONNY

Q *HOW MANY ANGELS DOES IT TAKE TO SCREW IN A LIGHT BULB?*

A *NONE, ANGELS ARE LIGHT*

- *DID YOU HEAR THE ONE ABOUT THE ANGEL WHO LOST THE NOTES FOR A SPEECH HE WAS GIVING AND HE HAD TO WING IT?*

- *I HAVE BEEN VISITING A SICK FRIEND OF MINE. HE HAD HARP FAILURE.*

- *I AM DELIGHTED THAT YOUR HOME CONTAINS SUCH A MEDITATIVE DEVICE. A TRUE SPIRITUAL CENTERPIECE!* *(Angel Sonny referring to the toilet.)*

Q *HOW MANY ANGELS CAN STAND ON THE HEAD OF A PIN?*

A *ALL OF US AT ONCE, SINCE WE TAKE UP NO SPACE. (BUT THEN ANGELS HAVE BETTER THINGS TO DO THAN GO AROUND STANDING ON THE HEADS OF PINS.)*

CONCLUSION

By Susan

We would like to take this opportunity to express our sincere gratitude to GOD, to Angel Sonny, to our Higher Selves, and to our Guardian Angels. Thank you all for everything; for all of the encouragement, for your patience with us when we have struggled, for lighting a fire under us when it was needed, and for <u>never</u> giving up on us. Thank you, also, for your understanding, compassion, and most of all, for the unconditional love you have shown us. We love you all very deeply!

Angel Sonny's book is now completed, but our new lives are just beginning. We now have forty new tools to take with us as we continue on our journey to the Light. We are by no means experts with the lessons, but as we continue to practice them, the more proficient we will all become. There have been many changes in our lives already and we feel many more just around the corner.

Bess works full time now, with the public, where she is able to practice her lessons on a daily basis. She looks at her job as an opportunity for accelerated growth and a chance to become an expert with the lessons. She realizes her job is a necessary step to living her higher path. In her spare time, she uses her gift of poetry. She writes beautiful, inspirational poems, some of which have been published already. Bess describes her life as, "Living a new life within my present one."

Pat has let go of many of her fears and has taken control of her life as never before. She explains it this way: "I have gone from being a meek little mouse, to a roaring lioness." She takes charge of her life and goes after what she wants. Pat has taken Sonny's advice and has gotten into touch healing. She is now a second degree Reiki practitioner. Bravo Pat!! She also has been working as a care giver for the elderly and disabled. Here she is able to enrich other people's lives while she enriches her own.

Chris has gained more confidence in seeing the value of his work. He has been painting beautiful pictures of some of the Peruvian children we have met on our travels. We are all very excited for him because he will be exhibiting them in an art show soon. He has started to manifest his dreams and realizes that he does have something of value to share with the world. The cover of this book, and the illustrations you find throughout it, are examples of how he plans to share his gifts. He says that when he uses his gifts, it truly does feel like 'Heaven on Earth' to him.

I have a wonderful job I truly love. I work with people who have handicaps in one form or another. What I have discovered, though, is that we all have 'handicaps', and as I work with them, helping them to overcome theirs, they work with me helping me to overcome mine. My job is a wonderful place to practice my lessons and to see the Light of God in all. I am also preparing to be a true, clear channel for the Angels. They have been giving me techniques to prepare me for the honor. I am very excited about it and I can hardly wait to get started. 'We' plan on writing another book with the information they will be giving me.

We are all learning to live more fully in the 'now'. We are learning to dream and to take steps, one at a time, in order to realize those dreams. We are learning more and more what it means to love ourselves, but when you are experiencing life with Angels, and feeling their love for you, you simply cannot help but love yourself a little more. It just happens. We are also learning to see the positive in all of our situations by using our lockets to gain more clarity and understanding.

The lessons in Angel Sonny's book have changed our lives in so many ways and it would take another book just to explain it all to you. Each day we are continuing to grow and more changes are taking place.

I would like to tell you about another very special Angel we have met. I will let Sonny introduce him in the same way he did to us. "*I WISH TO TELL YOU A LITTLE STORY ABOUT A FRIEND OF MINE. THROUGHOUT THE MANY CENTURIES, IN WHICH ENGLISH HAS*

BEEN SPOKEN, THERE HAS ALWAYS BEEN AN ANGEL, TO WHOM STORY-TELLERS HAVE ALWAYS ACKNOWLEDGED, BY BEGINNING EACH STORY WITH HIS NAME. YOU MAY HAVE HEARD HIS NAME MENTIONED, EVEN TODAY, ALWAYS AT THE START OF A BEAUTIFUL TALE. HIS LOVING INFLUENCE HAS HELPED ALL STORIES HAVE A HAPPY ENDING. AND SO I PRESENT HIM TO YOU, TO GUIDE YOUR EVERY NEW STORY BEGINNING, IN THE MANY TO BE EPISODES OF YOUR LIFE. DO YOU KNOW HIS NAME YET? HE IS ALWAYS MENTIONED AT THE START OF EVERY STORY - WUNTZA PONNATYME. SO CALL ON HIM WHEN YOU START A NEW CHAPTER IN YOUR LIFE. WE GO WAY BACK. OFTEN GOD TAKES THE TIME TO SIT AND SHOOT THE BREEZE WITH OLD WUNTZA BECAUSE HE KNOWS SO MANY GREAT STORIES." Wuntza has helped me put this book together and I would like to take this opportunity to thank him, as well.

May God's Love be with you as you
continue on your journey to the Light

Susan

MY CONCLUSION

By Angel Sonny

MY MISSION IS COMPLETE NOW THAT THIS BOOK IS IN YOUR HANDS. THE UNIVERSE IS REJOICING BECAUSE YOU CHOSE TO GROW AND CREATE YOUR HEAVEN ON EARTH. REALIZE THE TRUTHS IN GOD'S TEN REMINDERS TO YOU. KNOW THAT GOD IS NOT 'OUT THERE' SOMEWHERE DOING STUFF TO YOU OR FOR YOU. GOD IS 'IN' YOU AND YOU ARE A LIGHT OF GOD. GOD AND HIS ANGELS CO-CREATE WITH YOU WHENEVER YOU ASK FOR HELP, MAKE CONSCIOUS CHOICES, LISTEN TO GUIDANCE AND TAKE THE NECESSARY STEPS. IT IS WELL WITHIN YOUR CAPABILITIES TO FULLY REALIZE EVERY DREAM YOU HAVE. IT IS MY FONDEST HOPE THAT THE LESSONS IN THIS BOOK BRING YOU TO A FULLER AND MORE JOYOUS CONNECTION WITH GOD, WITH YOURSELF, YOUR HIGHER SELF, YOUR GUARDIAN ANGEL, OTHER PEOPLE, THE PLANET, AND THE WORLD. IT IS ALSO MY HOPE THAT YOU FEEL YOU BELONG AND HAVE A PURPOSE. YOU ARE IMPORTANT, YOU HAVE VALUE, AND YOU ARE LOVED. MAY GOD BLESS YOU AND HOLD YOU TENDERLY IN HIS LOVING ARMS.

WITH LOVE AND LIGHT,

SONNY

'The Fabulous Four'
Pat, Chris, Susan, and Bess

We hope you enjoyed reading Sonny's book and doing his lessons. We encourage groups to form to do the lessons and we would cherish and appreciate any letters from our readers, our co-creators of Heaven on Earth.

Angelic Mission Publishing
P. O. Box 16781
Portland, OR 97216

A B C D E F G
H I J K L M
N O P Q R S T
U V W X Y Z
ANGEL TALK
Copyright 1988 by INNER SEARCH